W9-BEA-468

ESTABLISHING A FREELANCE INTERPRETATION BUSINESS:

PROFESSIONAL GUIDANCE FOR SIGN LANGUAGE INTERPRETERS

THIRD EDITION

Tammera J. Richards, BS, CI & CT; SC:L; NAD IV

© 2008 Butte Publications, Inc.

Third Edition

Editor: Dorothy Taylor
Cover and Page Design: Anita Jones, Another Jones Graphics

All rights reserved. No part of this publication may be reproduced or transmitted in any form or by any means without permission in writing from the publisher.

This book is not intended to provide tax advice. As conditions and regulations vary by location and change over time, the reader is advised to consult an attorney and accountant for appropriate and detailed advice regarding the specifics of the reader's own business. The publisher makes no warranties, express or implied, regarding the accuracy, currency or reliability of the contents of this book regarding legal or tax matters. The publisher assumes no liability for the consequences of actions based upon the contents of this book.

ISBN: 978-1-884362-84-2

Butte Publications, Inc.
PO Box 1328
Hillsboro, OR 97123-1328
USA

Printed in the USA

TABLE OF CONTENTS

DEDICATION

To C.P.
Thank You!

Without the support of the following individuals, I would not be so fortunate as to see this book in its third edition. Please accept my heartfelt gratitude and appreciation.

Stefan N. Richards, MBA
Brian Goff, Ph.D.
Deborah Perry, MA, CI & CT
Jean A. Miller, CI & CT
Brenda J. Bentley, CI & CT
Elizabeth Morgan, MA, CI & CT; SC:L; NAD V; NIC IV
Laurie Meyer, MA, CSC, CI & CT

INTRODUCTION/FOREWORD

I became involved in the Deaf and interpreting communities in 1988. Within three years of graduation in 1992 from the Portland Community College Sign Language Interpretation Program (PCC SLIP), I was asked to write the first edition of this book which was published in 1995. The second edition (only slightly changed) was published in 1998. It is now 2008, and this year marks the 10-year anniversary of the second edition. It also marks the 19th year I have been involved in the field of sign language interpreting.

Looking back, I can't believe the amazing changes the field of interpreting has experienced in the last ten years. Some of the most memorable include:

- The creation and amazing proliferation of Video Relay Services.
- Modifications to the prerequisites required to sit for the Registry of Interpreters for the Deaf (RID) national certification evaluations.
- The collaborative innovation of the new National Interpreter Certification (NIC) evaluation by the RID and National Association of the Deaf (NAD).
- An enormous increase in the number of interpreters who are members of RID.
- Overhaul and improvement of the RID Code of Ethics resulting in the new RID Code of Professional Conduct (CPC).
- Continued rampant demand outpacing the supply of qualified sign language interpreters in community, educational, and video relay service settings.
- Incredible innovation in the telecommunications and computing industries allowing interpreters to take advantage of tools like text messaging, e-mail, instant messaging, video phone technology, global positioning systems (GPS), and other technical marvels.

One of the facets of interpreting that I find most gratifying and most stimulating is the fact that the field of interpreting is ever changing. This dynamic feature brings me great satisfaction when considering the diversity of work I am fortunate enough to do. The best part of this job is that I never consider myself "done" learning. An interpreter is always a work in progress, and having the attitude that there is always room for lifelong learning and improvement will only make you better at what you do. As a colleague once aptly put it, "In our field there is no ceiling!"

Another thing I have learned over the years since this book was originally published is that it is okay not to be an expert in everything. Two of the top skills an interpreter can develop are knowing whom to consult in order to get needed information, and being able to assess what he or she knows and doesn't know.

I would like to take this opportunity to thank the following individuals for their invaluable contributions to this book. Without their knowledge, insight, and expertise, this publication would not be nearly as valuable to interpreting professionals.

- Michael Harvey, Ph.D., A.B.P.P. - Dr. Harvey is the Co-Director of a private, non-profit organization, Dialogue Toward Change, located in Framingham, MA. This organization is dedicated to providing research, training and consultation services to alleviate the potentially negative impact of witnessing oppression. He earned his Ph.D. in Clinical Psychology from the University of South Dakota in 1978, and has been a psychologist in private practice specializing in deafness and hearing loss since 1980. In addition to over 40 articles, his publications include *The Odyssey of Hearing Loss: Tales of Triumph; Psychotherapy with Deaf and Hard of Hearing Persons: A Systemic Model (second edition);* and a co-edited book entitled *Culturally Affirmative Psychotherapy with Deaf Persons.* His most recent book is *Listen with the Heart: Relationships and Hearing Loss.* For more information go to: http://www.michaelharvey-phd.com

- Stefan N. Richards, MBA – Mr. Richards currently works as a Product Marketing Engineer for Intel Corporation. Mr. Richards has held a wide variety of business and technical roles at startup companies, as well as both Microsoft and Intel. Mr. Richards provides individual success coaching to technology professionals, as well as freelance business, technical, and financial consulting in a wide variety of settings. In addition to obtaining a Bachelor of Science in Computer Science from Oregon State University, Mr. Richards earned a Master of Business Administration at the University of Washington's renowned Technology Management MBA Program. Mr. Richards also earned a

Certificate in Financial Planning from the University of Portland in Portland, Oregon.

- Laurie Meyer, MA, CSC, CI & CT - Ms. Meyer has been a professional interpreter for more than 20 years. She has been extremely active in the New Hampshire and greater New England Deaf and interpreting communities, and currently is establishing new roots in the Pacific Northwest. Ms. Meyer has been instrumental in putting to use the Ally Model of interpreting, and has worked hard to develop relationships and foster understanding between Deaf consumers and interpreters through development of Allies Conferences held around the United States.

- Patrick Q. Fischer – Mr. Fischer, who has been Deaf since birth, has been a professional commercial and fine artist for over 15 years. He graduated from Portland Community College with his Associate of Applied Sciences Degree in Commercial Art in 1990. In addition, Mr. Fischer is an accomplished professional actor, performing in theatrical productions across the United States with the National Theatre for the Deaf. Currently, Patrick divides his time between teaching American Sign Language, working on various graphic design contracts, and entertaining people with his one-man performance and educational program called Mr. Shineyhead. For more information on Patrick's services, see his websites: http://www.mrshineyhead.com and http://www.idwiz.com

ONE

The History of Sign Language Interpreting

THOUGH THE INTENT of this book is not to describe comprehensively the evolution of the interpreting field, it is important that professional interpreters have an understanding of how this field came into being. The following section will discuss the origins of sign language interpreting, the historically prevalent models of interpreting, types of certification awarded by the Registry of Interpreters for the Deaf and other entities, and the impact of video relay services (VRS) on the profession of sign language interpreting.

It is well known that the first sign language "interpreters" weren't "professional" interpreters, but children born to Deaf parents (also called children of Deaf adults or CODAs). By virtue of their status as hearing intermediaries sharing a native Deaf culture and the language of ASL with their parents, they have been and often continue to be relied upon to provide communication access to their Deaf parents and the Deaf Community. Historically, these children were asked to provide this type of "interpreting" service to their parents at a very early age, and in unlimited types of settings. As the profession of interpreting has evolved, this practice has decreased but has by no means been eliminated.

Prior to the 1960's, the literature about sign language and interpreting made no distinction between "helpers" (hearing people who were willing to help sign with a deaf person) and "interpreters." (Frishberg, p.11).

In 1964, at Ball State Teacher's College in Muncie, Indiana, a workshop for rehabilitation personnel, educators, and interpreters was held. During this conference, the concept of a national professional organization for interpreters was proposed. It was then that the National Registry of Interpreters for the Deaf (RID) was conceived and developed. During the conference, it was agreed that a code of ethics would be developed, as well as a constitution for the new organization (Frishberg, p.12). The establishment of the RID was initially funded by a grant from the Rehabilitation Services Administration (RSA) administered through the National Association of the Deaf (NAD). The initial goals of the founders of the RID were to maintain and distribute a registry of accredited interpreters, establish certification standards for qualified interpreters, recruit qualified interpreters, educate qualified interpreters, and prepare literature relating to the methodology and problems of interpreting (Frishberg, p.13). Currently, RID boasts over 10,000 members worldwide, and has gone through three different iterations of interpreter evaluation and certification.

There are now more than 172 programs offering either certificates of completion, Associate's, Bachelor's, or Master's Degrees in Sign Language Interpretation. Initially, there were six institutions that received federal funding in the form of a 5-year grant (which was later renewed for an additional five years) from the RSA to establish interpreter training programs. These entities were: California State University at Northridge, Gallaudet College, New York University, St. Paul (MN) Technical Vocational Institute, Seattle (WA) Central Community College, and the University of Tennessee at Knoxville (Frishberg, pp.13-14).

The need for qualified, skilled interpreters has continued to outpace supply. The skills interpreters must possess in order to be successful mean that a great deal of time and effort must go into developing and educating them. Institutions providing programs in sign language interpretation often have met with difficulties in funding because of the low number of graduates turned out each year. Research indicates that everyone pursuing the career cannot develop interpreting skills. The ability of sign language interpretation programs to produce enough interpreters to address the demand will continue to be an issue as the incidence of deafness in the population maintains its level and the proliferation of video relay services and establishment of large call centers pull interpreters out of the community into full-time positions.

The need for professional interpreting services was first recognized in legislation with the Vocational Rehabilitation Act Amendments of 1965 (Public Law 89-333), followed by the Rehabilitation Act of 1973 and the Education for All Handicapped Children Act (Public Law 94-142) of 1975.

The most recent laws pertaining to the provision of qualified interpreters are the Americans with Disabilities Act (ADA) of 1990 and the revision of PL-94-142, now known as the Individuals with Disabilities Education Act (IDEA).

These laws specify provision of access to **qualified** sign language interpreters as a reasonable accommodation by public entities (Title 3 of the ADA), employers (Title 2 of the ADA), and state and local government entities (Title 1 of the ADA), as well as by public, K-12, educational settings (IDEA). Federal entities and those entities that receive federal funding are governed under sections 501-504 of the Rehabilitation Act of 1973. It is important to note that even after the passage of numerous pieces of legislation, **certified** interpreters are not currently mandated by these laws, and legislative language continues to use the ambiguous word "qualified." These laws say little or nothing about who determines whether an interpreter is "qualified."

INTERPRETING MODELS: A RETROSPECTIVE

Over the last 40 years, the field of sign language interpretation has grown and developed into a booming profession with thousands of practitioners across the United States and Canada. It is not surprising that as the field has grown, the model for the practice of interpreting has changed and evolved. The following section will examine the various interpreting models that have been used since interpreting became a profession.

The Helper Model of Interpreting

In the early stages of the field, the interpreting model we now call the Helper model was influenced by the natural interpreting done by hearing children of Deaf parents (CODAs) for family and friends. The Helper model reflected a time before American Sign Language (ASL) was widely recognized as a language and prior to the implementation of an interpreter training network. In addition to CODAs, interpreters working during this period came out of religious settings and/or were faculty members at schools for the Deaf.

The Helper model is often described as interpreters viewing Deaf people as dependent or needy and is frequently held up as an example of how NOT to interpret. The blurred boundaries between Deaf people and interpreters during this period had an impact on the development of the Code of Ethics.

The period during which this model was used is not without merit. Interpreters were creating a profession, often in collaboration with Deaf people. Consequently, flexibility became available to Deaf people through access to professional interpreters.

As with all models of interpreting, it is important to remember that a critical component to providing appropriate services is to meet the Deaf person at his or her level of competence in order to facilitate achievement of his or her goal(s).

The Conduit/Machine Model of Interpreting

In reaction to the impact of the Helper model, and after the establishment of RID at the Ball State Teachers' Conference in Muncie, Indiana in the 1960's, practicing interpreters shifted to a model of interpreting known as the Conduit or Machine Model of interpreting. In this model, interpreters attempted invisibility and neutrality. They viewed themselves as a neutral, invisible conduit of information with the intent of returning control of the communication event to the Deaf person.

The difficulty with this model was that the interpreters ceased to recognize their impact on the setting, and often ceased to take responsibility for the intelligibility of the message. This period in our field is often remembered as a time when complete communication breakdowns could happen over something as simple as "tell him...tell her." For example, an uninitiated hearing consumer might say to the interpreter, "Tell him that his next paycheck will come out on Friday." Rather than the interpreter (or Deaf consumer) explaining that the hearing person should simply speak directly to the Deaf person in first person (e.g., "Your next paycheck will come out next Friday."), the interpreter would simply interpret to the Deaf person, "Tell-him, his next paycheck will come out next Friday." This lack of mediation caused untold confusion on the part of both the Deaf and hearing consumers. The model assumed that conveying words in either ASL or English was sufficient for there to be effective communication. Deaf people received a representation of words spoken, but not necessarily an equivalent meaning of the message.

Interpreters, in attempting to be neutral, had trouble addressing issues related to the interpreting process that should be addressed by the interpreter rather than the Deaf consumer, such as explaining differences between ASL and

English, or explaining the interpreting process to a first-time interpreting consumer. This period was marked by a distancing between Deaf people and interpreters.

The Code of Ethics and professional standards were developed in response to these starkly contrasting models in an attempt to provide guidance to interpreters.

The Communication Facilitator Model of Interpreting

In this model, interpreters and Deaf people realized that previous models were not working. Interpreters began to assume responsibility for logistical issues such as lighting, seating, and checking in with the Deaf consumer prior to the assignment. While all of these things were positive changes, ultimately, interpreters were still not taking responsibility for successful communication. (Bar-Tzur, p. 2)[1]

The Bi-Lingual Bi-Cultural Mediator Model of Interpreting

The goal of this model was cultural equivalence by the interpreter for both the Deaf and hearing individuals involved in a communication event. This would allow the interpreter to facilitate successful communication for his or her consumers while taking into consideration each consumer's culture, perceptions, and prejudices. While this goal was admirable, it was very difficult if not inappropriate for the interpreter to assume expertise in one or both cultures, especially if either or both consumers were of a different ethnicity than the interpreter. Often, an attempt to be everything to everyone ends up leaving the interpreter with few boundaries and resentful consumers. While this model was positive in the sense that it fostered greater semantic message equivalency in ASL on the part of interpreters, it had the dangerous potential of being viewed as a "double helper" model. (Bar-Tzur, p.2).

The Ally Model of Interpreting

The Ally model of interpreting, while a much newer and somewhat novel approach, is becoming more widespread. It incorporates aspects of several of the other interpreting models, and simultaneously attempts to decrease if not eliminate any oppressive behaviors on the part of the interpreter towards the Deaf consumer. Generally, these oppressive behaviors are unintentional on the part of the interpreter, but by virtue of the interpreter

---

[1] Bar-Tzur, David http://www.theinterpretersfriend.com/misc/models.html p. 2

being a hearing person, oppression is bound to occur. One global example of oppressive interpreter behavior towards Deaf people is simply the belief that the interpreter knows what is best for the Deaf consumer, knows more than the Deaf consumer, or is responsible for taking care of the Deaf person to facilitate a certain outcome (paternalism). A more concrete, if not simplistic, example would be an interpreter deciding where a Deaf consumer sits during an interaction, rather than asking for the Deaf consumer's seating preference before beginning to work. A Brazilian educator named Paulo Freire, who wrote the book *Pedagogy of the Oppressed*, originally conceived the idea of the Ally Model. His belief is that power is shared by those who find strength and purpose in a common vision (allies). Collegiality, therefore, is based on shared and equal participation of all its members. One meaning of being an ally while interpreting is for the interpreter to avoid inadvertently oppressing Deaf people by perpetuating some of the built-in features of mainstream (Hearing) culture in which they were raised. (Bar-Tzur, pp. 3-4)

When applied to the interpreting profession, one example of the Ally Model in action is the open process model used during team interpreting assignments. See Chapter Five, Developing Yourself and Your Business, for further description of the open process model. While it would take an entirely separate book to detail the characteristics of the Ally model, one of the central themes seems to be the interpreter attempting to view the world with a "Deaf heart." The Ally model is an emerging model, within which Deaf people and interpreters together may determine how to function as allies.

CERTIFICATION OF SIGN LANGUAGE INTERPRETERS

As mentioned previously, the Registry of Interpreters for the Deaf (RID) was initially created with a primary goal of establishing certification evaluations and credentials for sign language interpreters. Over the past 40+ years, the certification evaluations given by RID have been revised three times resulting in varied testing designs, forms of implementation, and an increased psychometric reliability. The original certification evaluations were given in front of a live panel, and the source materials were on reel-to-reel film, while currently, the test is given at local testing sites throughout the United States, video taped, and shipped to individual raters around the country. In addition, the source material is provided on DVD. The following is a list of certificates awarded in the past and currently by RID, as well as additional certifications recognized by RID as valid credentials, although they are not conferred by RID.

First Generation RID Certification

CSC (Comprehensive Skills Certificate)

Holders of this full certificate have demonstrated the ability to interpret between American Sign Language (ASL) and spoken English, and to transliterate between spoken English and an English-based sign language. Holders of this certificate are recommended for a broad range of interpreting and transliterating assignments. The CSC examination was offered until 1987. **This test is no longer available.**

MCSC (Master Comprehensive Skills Certificate)

The MCSC examination was designed to test for a higher standard of performance than the CSC. Holders of this certificate were required to hold the CSC prior to taking this exam. Holders of this certificate are recommended for a broad range of interpreting and transliterating assignments. **This test is no longer available.**

RSC (Reverse Skills Certificate)

Holders of this full certificate have demonstrated the ability to interpret between American Sign Language (ASL) and English-based sign language or transliterate between spoken English and a signed code for English. Holders of this certificate are deaf or hard-of-hearing and interpretation/transliteration is rendered in ASL, spoken English and a signed code for English or written English. Holders of the RSC are recommended for a broad range of interpreting assignments where the use of an interpreter who is deaf or hard-of-hearing would be beneficial. **This test is no longer offered. Individuals interested in this certificate should take the CDI exam (see below).**

IC/TC (Interpretation Certificate/Transliteration Certificate)

Holders of this partial certificate demonstrated the ability to transliterate between English and a signed code for English and the ability to interpret between American Sign Language (ASL) and spoken English. These individuals received CSC examination scores that prevented the awarding of full CSC certification. **This test is no longer offered.**

IC (Interpretation Certificate)

Holder of this partial certificate demonstrated the ability to interpret between American Sign Language (ASL) and spoken English. This individual received scores on the CSC examination that prevented the awarding of full CSC certification or partial IC/TC certification. The IC was formerly known as the Expressive Interpreting Certificate (EIC). **This test is no longer offered.**

TC (Transliteration Certificate)

Holders of this partial certificate demonstrated the ability to transliterate between spoken English and a signed code for English. These individuals received CSC examination scores that prevented the awarding of full CSC certification or IC/TC certification. The TC was formerly known as the Expressive Transliterating Certificate (ETC). **This test is no longer offered.**

Second Generation RID Certification

CI (Certificate of Interpretation)

Holders of this certificate are recognized as fully certified in interpretation and have demonstrated the ability to interpret between American Sign Language (ASL) and spoken English for both sign-to-voice and voice-to-sign tasks. The interpreter's ability to transliterate is not considered in this certification. Holders of the CI are recommended for a broad range of interpretation assignments. **This test is available until December 2008.**

CT (Certificate of Transliteration)

Holders of this certificate are recognized as fully certified in transliteration and have demonstrated the ability to transliterate between English-based sign language and spoken English for both sign-to-voice and voice-to-sign tasks. The transliterator's ability to interpret is not considered in this certification. Holders of the CT are recommended for a broad range of transliteration assignments. **This test is available until December 2008.**

CI and CT (Certificate of Interpretation and Certificate of Transliteration)

Holders of both full certificates (as listed above) have demonstrated competence in both interpretation and transliteration. Holders of the CI and CT are recommended for a broad range of interpretation and transliteration assignments.

CDI (Certified Deaf Interpreter)
Holders of this certification are interpreters who are deaf or hard-of-hearing, and who have completed at least eight hours of training on the NAD-RID Code of Professional Conduct; eight hours of training on the role and function of an interpreter who is deaf or hard-of-hearing; and have passed a comprehensive combination of written and performance tests. Holders of this certificate are recommended for a broad range of assignments where an interpreter who is deaf or hard-of-hearing would be beneficial. **This test is currently available.**

OIC:C (Oral Interpreting Certificate: Comprehensive)
Holders of this generalist certificate demonstrated both the ability to transliterate a spoken message from a person who hears to a person who is deaf or hard-of-hearing and the ability to understand and repeat the message and intent of the speech and mouth movements of the person who is deaf or hard-of-hearing. **This test is no longer offered. Individuals interested in oral certification should take the OTC exam.**

OIC:S/V (Oral Interpreting Certificate: Spoken to Visible)
Holders of this partial certificate demonstrated the ability to transliterate a spoken message from a person who hears to a person who is deaf or hard-of-hearing. This individual received OIC:C examination scores that prevented the awarding of full OIC:C certification. **This test is no longer offered. Individuals interested in oral certification should take the OTC exam.**

OIC:V/S (Oral Interpreting Certificate: Visible to Spoken)
Holders of this partial certificate demonstrated the ability to understand the speech and silent mouth movements of a person who is deaf or hard-of-hearing and to repeat the message for a hearing person. These individuals received OIC:C examination scores that prevented the awarding of full OIC:C certification. **This test is no longer offered. Individuals interested in oral certification should take the OTC exam noted below.**

OTC (Oral Transliteration Certificate)
Holders of this generalist certificate have demonstrated, using silent oral techniques and natural gestures, the ability to transliterate a spoken message from a person who hears to a person who is deaf or hard-of-hearing. They also have demonstrated the ability to understand and repeat the message

and intent of the speech and mouth movements of the person who is deaf or hard-of-hearing. **This test is currently available.**

National Association of the Deaf (NAD) Certification

- **NAD III (Generalist) - Average Performance**
  Holders of this certificate possess above average voice-to-sign skills and good sign-to-voice skills or vice versa. These individuals have demonstrated the minimum competence needed to meet generally accepted interpreter standards. Occasional words or phrases may be deleted but the expressed concept is accurate. The individual displays good control of the grammar of the second language and is generally accurate and consistent, but is not qualified for all situations.

- **NAD IV (Advanced) - Above Average Performance**
  Holders of this certificate possess excellent voice-to-sign skills and above average sign-to-voice skills or vice versa. These individuals have demonstrated above average skill in any given area. Performance is consistent and accurate. Fluency is smooth, with little deleted, and the viewer has no question as to the candidate's competency. With this certificate, an individual should be able to interpret in most situations.

- **NAD V (Master) - Superior Performance**
  Holders of this certificate possess superior voice-to-sign skills and excellent sign-to-voice skills. This individual has demonstrated excellent to outstanding ability in any given area. There are minimum flaws in their performance, and they have demonstrated interpreting skills necessary in almost all situations.

Current NIC Certification (National Interpreter Certification)

Individuals achieving certification at the NIC, NIC Advanced or NIC Master level are all professionally certified interpreters. The National Interpreter Certification (NIC) exam tests interpreting skills and knowledge in three critical domains:

1. General knowledge of the field of interpreting through the NIC Knowledge exam

2. Ethical decision making through the interview portion of the NIC Performance test

3. Interpreting and transliterating skills through the performance portion of the test.

In all three domains, certificate holders must demonstrate professional knowledge and skills that meet or exceed the minimum professional standards necessary to perform in a broad range of interpretation and transliteration assignments. Individuals who achieve any of the three NIC certification levels are to be commended.

- **NIC**
  Individuals who achieve the NIC level have passed the NIC Knowledge exam. They also have scored within the standard range of a professional interpreter on the interview and performance portions of the test.

- **NIC Advanced**
  Individuals who achieve the NIC Advanced level have passed the NIC Knowledge exam; scored within the standard range of a professional interpreter on the interview portion; and scored within the high range on the performance portion of the test.

- **NIC Master**
  Individuals who achieve the NIC Master level have passed the NIC Knowledge exam. They have scored within the high range of a professional interpreter on both the interview and performance portions of the test.

From the beginning of the test development process, under the mandate of the NAD-RID National Council on Interpreting (NCI), the subject matter experts on the test development committee were given the task of developing a test that "raised the bar" for ASL/English interpreting and transliterating standards. This resulted in the development of a challenging NAD-RID NIC test.

Passing the test at the NIC level indicates that the interpreter has demonstrated skills in interpreting that meet a standard professional performance level and should be able to perform the varied functions of interpreting on a daily basis with competence and skill. It also shows that an individual has passed a test with both interpreting and transliterating elements, as opposed to one or the other.

With increasingly higher standards for the NIC Advanced and NIC Master levels of the test, progressively fewer individuals will meet these requirements. Achieving either the Advanced or Master level is an accomplishment and indicates that the individual exceeds the professional standards established in most routine interpreting assignments. Individuals holding the NIC Advanced and/or Master level certifications may be expected to perform competently in all routine interpreting assignments as well as in assignments that may be more complex in nature or that require interpreting skills above standard levels. (http://www.rid.org/education/edu_certification/index.cfm/AID/45)

EIPA – The Educational Interpreter Performance Assessment

As of Fall 2006, RID began to recognize individuals who passed the Educational Interpreter Performance Assessment (EIPA) written and performance tests at the level of 4.0 or higher as certified members of RID. Levels 4 and 5 of the EIPA are described below. Currently, more than 25 states recognize and/or require educational interpreters to be certified under the EIPA system. EIPA testing will continue to be administered by Boys Town and will be monitored by RID to ensure a continued maintenance of validity and reliability. For more information about EIPA testing, go to http://www.classroominterpreting.org/EIPA/performance/index.asp.

Level 4: Advanced Intermediate
Demonstrates broad use of vocabulary with sign production that is generally correct. Demonstrates good strategies for conveying information when a specific sign is not in their vocabulary. Grammatical constructions are generally clear and consistent, but complex information may still pose occasional problems. Prosody is good, with appropriate facial expression most of the time. May still have difficulty with the use of facial expression in complex sentences and adverbial non-manual markers. Fluency may deteriorate when rate or complexity of communication increases. Uses space consistently most of the time, but complex constructions or extended use of discourse cohesion may still pose problems. Comprehension of most signed messages at a normal rate is good but translation may lack some complexity of the original message.

An individual at this level would be able to convey much of the classroom content but may have difficulty with complex topics or rapid turn taking.

Level 5: Advanced

Demonstrates broad and fluent use of vocabulary, with a broad range of strategies for communicating new words and concepts. Sign production errors are minimal and never interfere with comprehension. Prosody is correct for grammatical, non-manual markers, and affective purposes. Complex grammatical constructions are typically not a problem. Comprehension of sign messages is very good, communicating all details of the original message. An individual at this level is capable of clearly and accurately conveying the majority of interactions within the classroom. (http://www.rid.org/UserFiles/File/pdfs/EIPA_FAQs.pdf)

ACCI – The American Consortium of Certified Interpreters

The ACCI test is the same test that carried the NAD label for a number of years. An agreement has been reached to give the option to those who have passed the ACCI test at levels III, IV or V to convert their certification to NAD certification and to allow them the opportunity to join RID under the same type of program that NAD interpreters were offered. Note: The levels of certification awarded by the ACCI are the same as the levels of certification listed above under "NAD Certification."

State Quality Assurance (QA) Certification Evaluations

Many states require professional interpreters to take and pass a state quality assurance evaluation in order to become a licensed interpreter and be able to provide interpreting services in those states. In order to determine whether or not your state has such a requirement, contact your local Commission for the Deaf and Hard-of-Hearing for details.

TWO

Ethical Considerations

THE REGISTRY OF INTERPRETERS FOR THE DEAF (RID), in conjunction with the National Association of the Deaf (NAD), developed the following guidelines for ethical conduct of sign language interpreters. Historically, RID began with its original Code of Ethics (CoE) which included expanded guidance for each tenet of the Code.

As the organization and profession of interpreting matured, the tenets of the Code remained the same, but the expanded guidance for each tenet was deleted. Finally, the current Code of Professional Conduct (CPC) was jointly developed by RID and NAD, and is the current ethical code by which members of RID are bound. This Code was formally adopted by RID on July 1, 2005 and is currently in effect.

The original Code of Ethics with the expanded guidance is shown below followed by the current Code of Professional Conduct.

ORIGINAL RID CODE OF ETHICS

- *Interpreters/transliterators shall keep all assignment-related information strictly confidential.*

  - **Guidelines:** Will not reveal information about any assignment, including the fact that the service is being performed. It only takes a minimum amount of information to identify the parties involved.

- *Interpreters/transliterators shall render the message faithfully, always conveying the content and spirit of the speaker using language most readily understood by the person(s) whom they serve.*

- **Guidelines:** Interpreters/transliterators are not editors and must transmit <u>everything</u> that is said in exactly the same way it was intended. This is especially difficult when the interpreter disagrees with what is being said, or feels uncomfortable when profanity is being used. Interpreters/transliterators must remember that they are not at all responsible for what is said, only for conveying it accurately. If the interpreter's/transliterator's own feelings interfere with rendering the message accurately, he/she shall withdraw from the situation.

- While working from spoken English to sign or non-audible spoken English, the interpreter/transliterator should communicate in the manner most easily understood or preferred by the deaf or hard-of-hearing person(s), be it American Sign Language (ASL), manually coded English, fingerspelling, paraphrasing in non-audible spoken English, gesturing, drawing, or writing. It is important for the interpreter/transliterator and deaf or hard-of-hearing person(s) to spend some time adjusting to each other's way of communicating prior to the actual assignment. When working from sign or non-audible spoken English, the interpreter/transliterator shall speak the language used by the hearing person in spoken form, be it English, Spanish, French, etc.

- *Interpreters/transliterators shall not counsel, advise or interject personal opinions.*

  - **Guidelines:** Just as interpreters/transliterators may not omit anything that is said, they may not add anything to what is said; they may not add anything to the situation, even when asked to do so by other parties involved.

- *An interpreter/transliterator is only present in a given situation because two or more people have difficulty communicating, and thus, the interpreter/transliterator's only function is to facilitate communication.* He/she shall not become personally involved because in so doing, he/she accepts some responsibility for the outcome, which does not rightfully belong to the interpreter/transliterator.

- *Interpreters/transliterators shall accept assignments using discretion with regard to skill, setting, and the consumers involved.*

  - **Guidelines:** Interpreters/transliterators shall only accept assignments for which they are qualified. However, when an interpreter/transliterator shortage exists, and the only available interpreter/transliterator does not possess the necessary skill for a particular assignment, this situation should be explained to the consumers.
  - If the consumers agree that services are needed regardless of the skill level, then the available interpreter/transliterator will have to use his/her best judgment about accepting or rejecting the assignment.
  - Certain situations may prove uncomfortable for some interpreters/transliterators and clients. Religious, political, racial or sexual difference, etc. can adversely affect the facilitating task. Therefore, an interpreter/transliterator shall not accept assignments that he/she knows will involve such inner conflict.

- *Interpreters/transliterators shall request compensation for services in a professional and judicious manner.*

  - **Guidelines:** Interpreters/transliterators shall be knowledgeable about fees that are appropriate to the profession.
  - There are circumstances when it is appropriate for interpreters/transliterators to provide services without charge. This should be done with discretion, taking care to preserve the self-respect of the consumers. Consumers should not feel that they are recipients of charity.

- *Interpreters/transliterators shall function in a manner appropriate to the situation.*

  - Guidelines: Interpreters/transliterators shall conduct themselves in such a manner that brings respect to themselves, the consumers, and the national organization. The term "appropriate manner" refers to (a) dressing in a manner that is appropriate for one's skin tone, and is not distracting and, (b) conducting oneself in all phases of an assignment in a manner befitting a professional.

- Interpreters/transliterators shall strive to further knowledge and skills through participation in workshops, professional meetings, interaction with professional colleagues, and reading of current literature in the field.
- Interpreters/transliterators, by virtue of membership or certification by the RID, Inc., shall strive to maintain high professional standards in compliance with the Code of Ethics.

CURRENT NAD-RID CODE OF PROFESSIONAL CONDUCT

The current NAD-RID Code of Professional Conduct can be accessed in its entirety on the RID website at: http://www.rid.org/ethics/code/index.cfm.

Tenets

1. Interpreters adhere to standards of confidential communication.

2. Interpreters possess the professional skills and knowledge required for the specific interpreting situation.

3. Interpreters conduct themselves in a manner appropriate to the specific interpreting situation.

4. Interpreters demonstrate respect for consumers.

5. Interpreters demonstrate respect for colleagues, interns, and students of the profession.

6. Interpreters maintain ethical business practices.

7. Interpreters engage in professional development.

Applicability

A. This Code of Professional Conduct applies to certified and associate members of the Registry of Interpreters for the Deaf, Inc., certified members of the National Association of the Deaf, interns, and students of the profession.

B. Federal, state or other statutes or regulations may supersede this Code of Professional Conduct. When there is a conflict between this code and local, state, or federal laws and regulations, the interpreter obeys the rule of law.

C. This Code of Professional Conduct applies to interpreted situations that are performed either face-to-face or remotely.

Definitions

For the purpose of this document, the following terms are used:

Colleagues: Other interpreters.

Conflict of Interest: A conflict between the private interests (personal, financial, or professional) and the official or professional responsibilities of an interpreter in a position of trust, whether actual or perceived, deriving from a specific interpreting situation.

Consumers: Individuals and entities that are part of the interpreted situation. This includes individuals who are deaf, deaf-blind, hard of hearing, and hearing.

Discussion of the Tenets of the NAD-RID Code

TENET 1.0 CONFIDENTIALITY: *Interpreters adhere to standards of confidential communication.*

Guiding principle: Interpreters hold a position of trust in their role as linguistic and cultural facilitators of communication. Confidentiality is highly valued by consumers and is essential to protecting all involved.

Each interpreting situation (e.g., elementary, secondary, and post-secondary education, legal, medical, mental health) has a standard of confidentiality. Under the reasonable interpreter standard, professional interpreters are expected to know the general requirements and applicability of various levels of confidentiality. Exceptions to confidentiality include, for example, federal and state laws requiring mandatory reporting of abuse or threats of suicide, or responding to subpoenas.

Illustrative behavior - Interpreters:

1.1   Share assignment-related information only on a confidential and "as-needed" basis (e.g., supervisors, interpreter team members, members of the educational team, hiring entities).

1.2   Manage data, invoices, records, or other situational or consumer-specific information in a manner consistent with maintaining consumer confidentiality (e.g., shredding, locked files).

1.3   Inform consumers when federal or state mandates require disclosure of confidential information.

TENET 2.0 PROFESSIONALISM: Interpreters possess the professional skills and knowledge required for the specific interpreting situation.

Guiding principle: Interpreters are expected to stay abreast of evolving language use and trends in the profession of interpreting as well as in the American Deaf community.

Interpreters accept assignments using discretion with regard to skill, communication mode, setting, and consumer needs. Interpreters possess knowledge of American Deaf culture and deafness-related resources.

Illustrative behavior - Interpreters:

2.1   Provide service delivery regardless of race, color, national origin, gender, religion, age, disability, sexual orientation, or any other factor.

2.2   Assess consumer needs and the interpreting situation before and during the assignment and make adjustments as needed.

2.3   Render the message faithfully by conveying the content and spirit of what is being communicated, using language most readily understood by consumers, and correcting errors discreetly and expeditiously.

2.4   Request support (e.g., certified deaf interpreters, team members, language facilitators) when needed to fully convey the message or to address exceptional communication challenges (e.g. cognitive disabilities, foreign sign language, emerging language ability, or lack of formal instruction or language).

2.5   Refrain from providing counsel, advice, or personal opinions.

2.6   Judiciously provide information or referral regarding available interpreting or community resources without infringing upon consumers' rights.

TENET 3.0 CONDUCT: *Interpreters conduct themselves in a manner appropriate to the specific interpreting situation.*

Guiding principle: Interpreters are expected to present themselves appropriately in demeanor and appearance. They avoid situations that result in conflicting roles or perceived or actual conflicts of interest.

Illustrative behavior - Interpreters:

3.1   Consult with appropriate persons regarding the interpreting situation to determine issues such as placement and adaptations necessary to interpret effectively.

3.2   Decline assignments or withdraw from the interpreting profession when not competent due to physical, mental, or emotional factors.

3.3   Avoid performing dual or conflicting roles in interdisciplinary (e.g. educational or mental health teams) or other settings.

3.4   Comply with established workplace codes of conduct, notify appropriate personnel if there is a conflict with this Code of Professional Conduct, and actively seek resolution where warranted.

3.5   Conduct and present themselves in an unobtrusive manner and exercise care in choice of attire.

3.6   Refrain from the use of mind-altering substances before or during the performance of duties.

3.7   Disclose to parties involved any actual or perceived conflicts of interest.

3.8   Avoid actual or perceived conflicts of interest that might cause harm or interfere with the effectiveness of interpreting services.

3.9   Refrain from using confidential interpreted information for personal, monetary, or professional gain.

3.10 Refrain from using confidential interpreted information for the benefit of personal or professional affiliations or entities.

TENET 4.0 RESPECT FOR CONSUMERS: *Interpreters demonstrate respect for consumers.*

Guiding principle: Interpreters are expected to honor consumer preferences in selection of interpreters and interpreting dynamics, while recognizing the realities of qualifications, availability, and situation.

Illustrative behavior - Interpreters:

4.1 Consider consumer requests or needs regarding language preferences, and render the message accordingly (interpreted or transliterated).

4.2 Approach consumers with a professional demeanor at all times.

4.3 Obtain the consent of consumers before bringing an intern to an assignment.

4.4 Facilitate communication access and equality, and support the full interaction and independence of consumers.

TENET 5.0 RESPECT FOR COLLEAGUES: *Interpreters demonstrate respect for colleagues, interns and students of the profession.*

Guiding principle: Interpreters are expected to collaborate with colleagues to foster the delivery of effective interpreting services. They also understand that the manner in which they relate to colleagues reflects upon the profession in general.

Illustrative behavior - Interpreters:

5.1 Maintain civility toward colleagues, interns, and students.

5.2 Work cooperatively with team members through consultation before assignments regarding logistics, providing professional and courteous assistance when asked and monitoring the accuracy of the message while functioning in the role of the support interpreter.

5.3 Approach colleagues privately to discuss and resolve breaches of ethical or professional conduct through standard conflict resolution methods; file a formal grievance only after such attempts have been unsuccessful or the breaches are harmful or habitual.

5.4 Assist and encourage colleagues by sharing information and serving as mentors when appropriate.

5.5 Obtain the consent of colleagues before bringing an intern to an assignment.

TENET 6.0 BUSINESS PRACTICES: *Interpreters maintain ethical business practices.*

Guiding principle: Interpreters are expected to conduct their business in a professional manner whether in private practice or in the employ of an agency or other entity. Professional interpreters are entitled to a living wage based on their qualifications and expertise. Interpreters are also entitled to working conditions conducive to effective service delivery.

Illustrative behavior - Interpreters:

6.1   Accurately represent qualifications, such as certification, educational background, and experience, and provide documentation when requested.

6.2   Honor professional commitments and terminate assignments only when fair and justifiable grounds exist.

6.3   Promote conditions that are conducive to effective communication, inform the parties involved if such conditions do not exist, and seek appropriate remedies.

6.4   Inform appropriate parties in a timely manner when delayed or unable to fulfill assignments.

6.5   Reserve the option to decline or discontinue assignments if working conditions are not safe, healthy, or conducive to interpreting.

6.6   Refrain from harassment or coercion before, during, or after the provision of interpreting services.

6.7   Render pro bono services in a fair and reasonable manner.

6.8   Charge fair and reasonable fees for the performance of interpreting services and arrange for payment in a professional and judicious manner.

TENET 7.0 PROFESSIONAL DEVELOPMENT: *Interpreters engage in professional development.*

Guiding principle: Interpreters are expected to foster and maintain interpreting competence and the stature of the profession through ongoing development of knowledge and skills.

Illustrative behavior - Interpreters:

7.1   Increase knowledge and strengthen skills through activities such as:
- pursuing higher education;
- attending workshops and conferences;
- seeking mentoring and supervision opportunities;
- participating in community events; and
- engaging in independent studies.

7.2   Keep abreast of laws, policies, rules, and regulations that affect the profession.

RID ETHICAL PRACTICES AND STANDARDS SYSTEM (EPS)

The Registry of Interpreters for the Deaf has worked hard to develop an Ethical Practices and Standards System that is used to attempt to resolve disputes between interpreters and consumers of interpreting services. The process for filing grievances against interpreters is defined within this system, and consists of a number of steps. It is important to note that unless an interpreter is an active member (and practicing interpreter) of RID, he/she cannot have grievances filed against him/her under this system.

The Ethical Practices and Standards process can be accessed in its entirety via the RID website at: http://www.rid.org/UserFiles/File/pdfs/EPS_Manual.pdf. In brief, the process of filing a grievance and resolving it is described below.

Grievance Process

1. Complaint submitted

A person files a complaint by filling out the Enforcement complaint filing form. The complainant provides information about the interpreter against whom they are filing, describes the incident and the alleged misconduct, and cites which tenets of the NAD-RID Code of Professional Conduct were violated. In addition, a detailed narrative must accompany the filing form.

2. Complaint reviewed

Each complaint is reviewed, and a determination is made as to whether the complaint will be pursued. Before a case can be accepted, the national office may request additional information.

3. Complaint dismissed

A complaint may be dismissed if the documentation is incomplete or if the complaint itself is non-actionable, non-substantive or has already been corrected by another means.

4. Complaint accepted

If a complaint is accepted, the complainant and respondent will receive letters that an official case has been opened.

The respondent is asked to submit a written response to the allegations. The response should include a detailed narrative and address each of the violations alleged in the complaint.

5. Mediation session

Mediation is a collaborative problem-solving process that allows the person filing the complaint and the interpreter to discuss a shared conflict and mutually agree upon a resolution. The parties meet with one or two mediators who serve as neutral third parties to facilitate and guide the discussion. Mediation is the first step in the multi-level grievance system. It aims to increase the efficiency with which complaints can be handled and to restore relationships.

6. Agreement

The parties may come together and discuss the basis of the complaint and possible ways to resolve it. If so, the parties each agree to follow the terms of the agreement. The hope is that they will clarify any misunderstandings, address the allegations of ethical misconduct and mutually agree on the best course of action to resolve it.

7. No agreement

The parties may reach an impasse or be unable to find an amicable solution that satisfies both sides. If that is the case, the mediator(s) will close the session and submit the case to the next level, which is adjudication. If a mediation agreement is reached but one or both of the parties does not meet the terms of the agreement, the case moves to adjudication.

8. Adjudication

Adjudication is a peer review process in which a selected panel of interpreters evaluates evidence of an alleged violation and determines whether a professional action was in violation of the NAD-RID Code of Professional Conduct. If it is determined that a violation did occur, the panel is further empowered to determine what sanctions should be imposed.

The role of the adjudication panel is to review official EPS cases and objectively weigh the issues of the complaint, the response and the supporting evidence. The panel relies on the information provided by the parties to determine the merits of the case, whether the interpreter's action constitutes a clear ethical breach, and what, if any, sanctions are warranted.

9. Violation

After careful review, the adjudication panel reviewing the complaint may find that the interpreter's behavior is a clear breach of the code. If that is the case, they will make a written declaration with a rationale for their decision. The panel will also decide what the interpreter must do in response to the violation. The decision-making power is in the hands of the panel assigned to the case.

10. No violation

After considering the facts and circumstances, the adjudication panel reviewing a case may find that the interpreter's behavior was not a breach of the code. They may decide that the evidence is inconclusive and render a decision of no violation. It is possible that the interpreter's behavior is unbecoming of an interpreter, but not an ethical breach against the code of conduct.

11. Appeal

After a panel of adjudicators renders a decision on a case, either party may file an appeal of that decision on the basis of the grounds laid out in the EPS policy manual. If it meets the requirements, a new panel of adjudicators will review the decision of the first panel.

12. Final decision

In the event that a case is not appealed, the panel's decision is final. If an appeal is filed and is accepted, the decision will be reviewed, but the appeal panel's decision is final as it is the last level of appeal in the process.

THREE

The Intricacies of Business

GOING INTO BUSINESS for yourself can be a confusing and intimidating prospect. Not to worry; it's really not that bad. A few important aspects are detailed in this chapter. The IRS, in Publication 583 – Starting a Business and Keeping Records, provides a good alternate resource for the basics. That publication covers much of the material included here in another form.

References:
IRS Publication 583 – Starting a Business and Keeping Records:
> http://www.irs.gov/publications/p583/index.html
> http://www.irs.gov/pub/irs-pdf/p583.pdf

BEING AN INDEPENDENT CONTRACTOR VERSUS AN EMPLOYEE

Working as a freelance interpreter is usually not the same as most typical employment. As a freelance interpreter, you usually work for yourself as an *independent contractor*. This has some significant and vital differences from being an employee.

How Do I Tell Which One I Am?

Your status may change from job to job. For example, you may be retained as a part-time staff interpreter at a school (typically as an employee) while continuing to take freelance jobs in the community as they come up (typically as an independent contractor). Below are some guidelines to help determine which situation you're in for any given position.

Signs that you're an employee
The following are all good indications (in some case definitive indications) that you are an employee:

- You work at the direction of someone else with little choice of what work you take or turn down, or how the work is to be completed
- You are provided with most of the resources needed to do your job by the person paying for service (e.g. a text pager, a computer, a printer, an internet connection, and/or an office)
- You submit an IRS W4 form to the person or organization paying you
- You receive an IRS W2 form from the person or organization that pays you at the end of the year
- You receive pay stubs with breakdowns of taxes and other deductions with your paychecks
- You don't have to create an invoice for (bill for) your hours worked

Signs that you're an independent contractor

The following are all good indications (in some case definitive indications) that you are an independent contractor:

- You fully control the work you accept and turn down
- You conduct your work using your own provided resources
- You submit an IRS W9 form to the person or organization paying you
- You receive an IRS 1099 form at the end of the year from the person or organization that pays you
- You receive checks, but no pay stubs with breakdowns of taxes or any other deductions
- You must periodically invoice (bill for) your hours worked in order to get paid

If you are unsure, references directly from the IRS provide a great deal more detail.

References:

IRS article on self-employed individuals versus independent contractors:
    http://www.irs.gov/businesses/small/article/0,,id=99921,00.html
IRS article on self-employed individuals:
    http://www.irs.gov/businesses/small/article/0,,id=115045,00.html
IRS Topic 762 – Independent Contractor vs. Employee:
    http://www.irs.gov/taxtopics/tc762.html

Why Is It So Important to Know the Difference?

The main reason is taxes. If you are an independent contractor, the responsibility to pay all taxes and withholdings on time is yours. If you're an employee, it's up to your employer to do this. This is no small matter. However, as an independent contractor, you do gain the ability to deduct a number of things from your income prior to paying taxes. Below is a discussion of deductible expenses and self-employment taxes.

Deductible expenses

Employees are heavily restricted in the deductions they may take for work expenses, since the employer is expected to provide most resources. As an independent contractor, many things you would typically just buy can be treated as an expense of running your business and deducted from your personal income taxes. IRS Publication 15, Circular E, covers many of the things that can and cannot be deducted as a legitimate business expense. IRS Publication 15B also contains good information about deductible fringe benefits.

Some examples of deductible business expenses include:
- Partial depreciation (or rent) for the portion of your home used as a dedicated home office, including deduction for the same portion of utilities (specifically covered in IRS Publication 587)
- Cost of special phone lines used solely for business purposes
- Purchase of office equipment for sole use in your business (like a computer used primarily for billing, advertising through the web, messaging with clients, bookkeeping and scheduling, or a fax machine used for faxing forms and invoices to clients)
- Direct expenses of fulfilling the main duties of your business (for example, the cost of paper, ink and postage for invoicing)
- Travel expenses to jobs (as long as the travel cannot be constituted as a regular commute)
- Certain other "fringe benefits," like discounts or dependent care assistance (specifically covered in IRS Publication 15B)

Caution must be taken not to get carried away with claiming business expenses. They must be legitimately tied to your creation of income and not easily mistakable for a personal asset just being used occasionally for business purposes. For more information, you should review IRS publication 15,

Circular E. Before assuming something is deductible, especially a big item, it is also highly advisable to discuss it with a tax professional or accountant.

References:
IRS Publication 15, Circular E – Employer's Tax Guide:
http://www.irs.gov/pub/irs-pdf/p15.pdf (publication)
http://www.irs.gov/publications/p15/index.html (web site)
IRS Publication 15B – Employer's Tax Guide to Fringe Benefits:
http://www.irs.gov/publications/p15b/index.html
IRS Publication 334 – Tax Guide for Small Business (Chapter 8 –
Business Expenses): http://www.irs.gov/publications/p334/ch08.html
IRS Publication 535 – Business Expenses:
http://www.irs.gov/publications/p535/index.html
IRS Publication 587 – Business Use of Your Home:
http://www.irs.gov/publications/p587/index.html

Self-employment taxes

As an independent contractor you must pay self-employment taxes. Self-employment taxes are payments to Social Security and Medicare/Medicaid federal programs, commonly referred to as the Federal Insurance Contributions Act, or FICA, taxes. The total amount paid in FICA for any working individual is 15.3% of net income, with limits on the Social Security portion when gross wages exceed a certain annual amount.

The good news is, as an independent contractor, you can usually deduct half of your FICA tax on your personal federal income taxes. This amount is the portion typically paid by an employer on behalf of an employee, which is why it is deductible (same as it would be deductible for a business paying this on behalf of its employees). That means half of that tax is paid with money before taxes are assessed, half after. The half after is the same as what you pay when you're an employee (commonly shows up on your pay stub as FICA, or separated out as Social Security and Employee Medicare on your pay stub).

The bad news is, you must pay all of your FICA taxes quarterly to the IRS.

In addition to FICA, you must also make estimated federal income tax payments. This is all done by way of IRS Form 1040-ES on a quarterly basis.

References:

IRS article on self-employment taxes:
http://www.irs.gov/businesses/small/article/0,,id=98846,00.html

IRS Article on estimated taxes:
http://www.irs.gov/businesses/small/article/0,,id=110413,00.html

IRS Publication 1518 - Tax calendar for Small Businesses and Self-Employed:
http://www.irs.gov/businesses/small/content/0,,id=168430,00.html
http://www.irs.gov/pub/irs-pdf/p1518.pdf

IRS Form 1040 Schedule SE – Self-employment Tax:
http://www.irs.gov/pub/irs-pdf/f1040sse.pdf

IRS Form 1040-ES – Estimated Tax for Individuals (quarterly filing):
http://www.irs.gov/pub/irs-pdf/f1040es.pdf

CHOOSING A BUSINESS STRUCTURE

Business Structures Defined

Going into business for yourself means you must make some decisions about the formal structure under which you will do business. There are four basic business structures typically recognized by state and federal governments in the United States. Only three are really practical for a freelance interpreting business.

Sole Proprietorship

A sole proprietorship is basically just you going into business as you. If you take no action to form any kind of other business structure, you are assumed to be a sole proprietor by the IRS. Despite not forming any kind of formal business structure, you still have significant responsibilities that can be very costly if not met.

Being a sole proprietor has some great advantages. It has the lowest amount of administrative overhead and the lowest cost to maintain of any business structure. No additional tax returns have to be filed for your business; all of your income and expenses are included on schedule C of IRS Form 1040.

However, being a sole proprietor does carry one major disadvantage. Because there is no separate business entity involved, you are personally liable for all actions of your business. This includes the actions of any employees of your business. That means a civil lawsuit against your business can attach your personal assets, such as your house, car, or savings. This is a huge exposure, although it may be mitigated by proper personal and/or business liability insurance.

References:
IRS Form 1040 Schedule C – Business Profit and Loss:
    http://www.irs.gov/pub/irs-pdf/f1040sc.pdf

Limited Liability Corporation (LLC)
Limited liability corporations, or LLCs, are a relatively new business structure created by statute at the state level. Not all states allow the forming of LLCs. The IRS does not formally recognize an LLC as a tax entity separate from the individual. To the IRS, an LLC looks like a sole proprietor. For this reason, all income and/or loss of the business is filed in your personal income tax returns on Schedule C of IRS Form 1040.

States that allow the forming of an LLC do recognize the LLC as an entity separate from the individual or individuals that form it. For this reason, states offer you some protection from claims against the business and its employees. Claims against an LLC or its employees are typically limited in that the claims can only attach the assets of the business, removing most of the personal liability from you and protecting your non-business assets from legal settlement actions. The exception is personal negligence. Persons or businesses that believe they incurred damages due to your personal negligence can always name you personally in a lawsuit. No form of business protects you from liability for personal negligence.

Because LLCs typically are seen as separate at the state level, states usually will require you to file tax documents for the business activity of your LLC on an annual or quarterly basis.

LLCs are a nice compromise between sole proprietorship and a corporation in that they offer the limited liability aspect of forming a separate business entity, but typically can be formed and maintained with very little administrative overhead and expense.

S-Corporation

S-Corporations were created in the absence of LLCs to allow smaller businesses to form corporations without the high administrative overhead and cost of forming a full-blown corporation (often referred to as a C-Corporation). An S-Corporation is a completely separate business entity, but all of its profits and losses flow directly through to the shareholders whether profits are distributed or not. For this reason, an S-Corporation typically does not pay any business taxes. The limited cases where S-Corporations do have to pay business taxes would not typically apply to an interpreter business.

This business structure gives you the feature of protection of your personal assets from most liability claims against the corporation, since you are seen as separate entities in the eyes of the law. The personal negligence exception still applies, as described above. The overhead and cost typically are higher than for an LLC.

Because an S-Corporation is recognized as a separate business entity, both state and federal returns must be filed for the business in addition to any returns filed by the owner or owners. However, as mentioned previously, all profits and losses flow through directly to the owners, so an S-Corporation typically does not pay federal income taxes (with a few exceptions).

C-Corporation

C-Corporations are those we typically envision when we think of a "corporation." Microsoft, GE, Ford Motors, and General Mills are all C-Corporations. This business form does not typically apply to freelance interpreters because the expense and administrative overhead involved make it undesirable and cost prohibitive.

Business Structures Compared

On the next page is a table comparing important aspects of each business structure. It is provided as a guide to help you in selecting an appropriate business structure.

Table 1.

Business Structure Summary

	Bookkeeping Required	Revenue & Expenses Affect Personal Income Taxes Due	State Business Entity Creation Required	Some Level of Liability Protection	Federal Corporate Income Tax Returns Required
Sole Propietor	✓	✓			
LLC	✓	✓	✓	✓	
S-Corp	✓	✓	✓	✓	✓

My Take on Business Structure

In my opinion, the best business structure for a freelance interpreter is either a sole proprietorship or an LLC. A sole proprietorship is the easiest to maintain, although it does have the downside of personal liability. If it is just you in business for yourself and you are carrying adequate insurance, the risk of liability is probably small enough to save the cost of the extra overhead. However, if you work in areas where liability risks are high, such as legal or medical settings, or you have any employees at all, having the extra protection of an LLC is well worth the small incremental investment in time and money to maintain. S-Corporations provide few benefits over LLCs, yet have the highest cost and administrative overhead. If you're considering an S-Corporation and your state supports LLCs, I recommend that most individuals opt for an LLC.

My business, Northwest American Sign Language Associates, Inc., is an S-Corporation. It is only so because it was formed when LLCs did not exist in Oregon. The annual overhead of filing federal business tax returns is significant with little real benefit, because the net gains are still ultimately taxed at our individual tax rate. There is additional overhead besides the annual federal corporate tax return, as I have to do formal payroll to myself each month, including calculating deductions for FICA, federal and state withholding. Were I to do it again, now that Oregon supports LLCs, I would form my business as an LLC.

BASICS OF ACCOUNTING

Most people grimace when you mention accounting. Unfortunately, as someone in business for yourself, you must understand some of the basic principles of accounting to keep yourself out of trouble with the IRS and state tax authorities.

NOTE: It is highly recommended that you seek professional advice of a Certified Public Accountant (CPA) for accounting and tax advice. The guidance stated here is from experience in business and should NOT be construed as professional advice from a certified accountant. That said, the text that follows might help you understand what your CPA is talking about!

Cash Basis versus Accrual Basis

In accounting, there are two very basic principles that you must understand to do accurate reporting properly for your business. These are the concepts of *Cash Basis* and *Accrual Basis* accounting.

Cash basis

Cash basis accounting is the most basic and intuitive of accounting methods. All of your accounting is done based on cash flowing into and out of your bank account or physically changing hands. Most people think of money as a physical thing you have or do not have, so this is the most obvious and approachable method of accounting.

With a cash basis, when you complete work, your income is not recognized from an accounting perspective until you are actually paid—cash into your account. The same is true for bills you pay; the expense is not realized from an accounting perspective until you actually pay the bill—cash out of your account.

This is simple, but can lead to some gross miscalculations from a planning perspective. For example, how do you plan for paying annual license or certification maintenance dues? From the accounting perspective, this would look like a one-time expense occurring at the same time once every year. However, from a planning perspective, you probably need to be saving a portion of your pay in reserve each month to pay these large annual expenses.

One might think, why not make my accounting match this planning? This is a great introduction to the *Accrual Basis* method of accounting.

Accrual basis

Accrual basis accounting is actually simpler than it sounds. Accrual based accounting is simply recording both income and expense when they are <u>accrued</u> rather than when they are realized, as is done in cash basis accounting.

With an accrual basis, when you complete work and bill for it, the revenue is recognized. It doesn't matter if/when you get paid, your accounting records show a gain in revenue at the moment of billing. The same is true for expenses. The expenses are accounted for as they are accrued, as opposed to when the actual check is written for the expense. For example, one twelfth of your annual dues would be accounted for each month as an accrual toward the amount due annually.

This might seem counter-intuitive – recognizing transactions before money physically changes hands – but it is actually more familiar than you think. If you keep a checkbook register, you maintain an accrual accounting system. Every time you record a deposit or check in the register, you are writing an original accounting record for a transaction that will be completed in the future. If you've ever had a deposited check held or a check that you wrote not tendered for a while, you must know this to be the case. Making your checkbook match your bank balance, or *reconciling accounts,* can be very frustrating when people don't deposit checks you've written to them! You have an accrual on your account that has not been actualized. The money is gone, but it still shows in your account.

I'm Not an Accountant; Why Do I Care?

Even though you're not an accountant, you still hold the ultimate responsibility for your own accounting of your revenue and expenses. The IRS does not accept the argument that you didn't know better. If the IRS ever audits you, this is what they will want to see. If you don't have it, you will not like the results.

When setting up your bookkeeping and filing business tax returns, you must declare your accounting method. Once you pick one, you should stick to it. Switching methods is very difficult to do properly and usually raises the attention of the IRS. If considering changing accounting methods, consult your CPA!

Bookkeeping

I am only in business for myself and don't make much. Do I really need to do "bookkeeping"? Yes, you absolutely must do bookkeeping. Every business must do bookkeeping; this is not optional.

What is bookkeeping?
Bookkeeping is simply keeping track of the money you earn and the expenses you incur. These entries need to be put in what accountants call "the book of original entry," also known as a ledger.

How do I "keep my books"?
Bookkeeping means keeping a ledger. A ledger is very simple, not unlike a check register for a checking account. It records the date, a description, and the amount of *debit or credit*. Debit and credit are just accounting terms for inflow (debit) and outflow (credit). You can keep your ledger in a bound book (where the term "bookkeeping" comes from), but most people today rely on software.

I highly recommend using software, as there will be other things you'll want to do with the data later, like tax calculation and profit/loss calculations. Software makes these derivative reports and calculations trivial and will save you lots of time and hassle. A great program that is easy to use for this is *Intuit's QuickBooks*. I have used this program in my business for years. I have found it straightforward and maintainable with minimal effort. For more info, see *QuickBooks'* website: http://quickbooks.intuit.com. The simplest version of their product typically will work for most interpreter businesses, although more advanced versions do help with invoices and payroll, so they are worth considering.

LICENSURE AND TAX CONSIDERATIONS

Interpreter Licensure

Check into state laws regarding licensure to provide sign language interpreting services. In some states, it is a requirement that you register with the state (and usually pay a fee) in addition to possibly having to provide proof of passage of a State QA evaluation at a given level, or proof of possession of RID certification. Each state is different, and may or may not require licensure. It is important to verify your state's requirements because if you provide services without the requisite licensure, you could be fined, or otherwise penalized. In some states it is illegal to call yourself a professional sign language interpreter without possession of a valid state license.

Business Licensure

Check with your state and local governments regarding the requirements for business licensure. In some states and municipalities, professionals are required to pay a fee and possess a valid business license that is usually renewed every year. Depending on your location, you may also be required to pay business and occupancy (B &O) taxes as well. Each state is different, so do your research!

Bank Accounts and Employer ID Numbers

Bank accounts

It is a very good practice to maintain a separate bank account for your business. This will help keep your business income and expenses separate from your personal income and expenses. It is also a good way to evaluate the financial health of your business. If your business funds are intermingled with your personal funds, it is very hard to track business success and to tease business expenses out from personal ones. Having separate bank accounts is particularly helpful should the IRS ever audit you.

In the same regard, it is also good to carry a credit line (credit card) for your business that is separate from your personal credit accounts.

Employer ID numbers

An employer identification number (EIN) is a tax ID number assigned by the IRS to a business. Typically, an S-Corporation or LLC will apply for an EIN. This enables you to separate your finances fully from your personal finances. The LLC EIN will be tied back to the owner's social security number (SSN) for tax purposes at the IRS. Sole proprietors typically do not get EINs, unless they have employees.

EINs are very important. They are typically required for opening a business bank account under your business name. Many entities contracting for services only want to deal with businesses and will ask for an EIN for payment and remit payment to your business name. Having an EIN ahead of time is a good idea for obvious reasons.

References:
IRS article on employee ID numbers:
   http://www.irs.gov/businesses/small/article/0,,id=98350,00.html
IRS Online Application for EIN:
   http://www.irs.gov/businesses/small/article/0,,id=102767,00.html

Important Tax Dates

There are so many tax relevant dates; it can be very hard to keep track of what must be filed when and what must be paid when. To help, Table 2 below summarizes some of these filing requirements for federal taxes.

Table 2.
Tax Filing Dates

Business Filings	Jan 15th	Jan 31st	March 15th	April 15th	April 30th	June 15th	July 31st	Sept 15th	Oct 31st
941 due		✓			✓		✓		✓
Employee FICA & withholding pmt due		✓			✓		✓		✓
FUTA deposit due (if>$500)		✓			✓		✓		✓
FUTA deposit due (if<$500 prev year)		✓							
940 due		✓							
W2 forms to employees		✓							
1099 forms to contractors		✓							
Personal Filings									
Individual Estimated Tax payment due	✓		✓			✓		✓	
Form 1040 due				✓					

References:
IRS Publication 1518 – Tax Calendar for Small Businesses and
   Self-Employed:
   http://www.irs.gov/businesses/small/content/0,,id=168430,00.html
   http://www.irs.gov/pub/irs-pdf/p1518.pdf

NOTE: many states follow the same schedule for requiring state withholding tax payments and business quarterly filings. Check your state for exact dates.

FOUR

Financial Considerations for Interpreters: Planning for the Future

RETIREMENT

I'm just starting out; why do I care about retirement? You need to care about retirement savings as soon as you can because of the *time value of money.* A little bit of money invested now is worth much more than a lot of money invested later. If you need to see the power of this, I highly recommend you research the concepts presented here.

Setting up a retirement savings program of some kind early, can also have the benefit of using the government's money to earn you interest. Sounds strange, but it's true. Tax deferred savings programs, like 401(k) plans or traditional IRAs, allow you to put money away tax deferred, allowing you to collect interest on both the money you would have paid the IRS in taxes and what you would have had left! These plans allow you to save money for retirement with a lower effect on immediate cash flow due to the reduction in taxable income today. A dollar saved reduces your cash flow less than one dollar!

Retirement plans are not just for people employed by big companies. Small businesses and sole proprietors can also set up retirement programs at a fairly low cost and with low administrative overhead. Setting up such plans allows you to potentially save more for retirement in a tax advantaged way than you could normally save in a traditional individual IRA, which is very limited in the amount you can contribute per year with tax advantages. These retirement plans include Simplified Employee Pensions (SEPs), Savings Incentive Match Plans for Employees (SIMPLEs), and typical qualified plans, like a 401(k). It is highly recommended that you talk with a CPA and/or certified financial planner (CFP) for help evaluating and/or setting up such retirement plans, as they can get complicated for a lay person.

References:

IRS Publication 560 – Retirement Plans for Small Business:
http://www.irs.gov/pub/irs-pdf/p560.pdf

IRS Article – Retirement Tips for Individuals:
http://www.irs.gov/retirement/participant/article/0,,id=133069,00.html

ABSENCE DUE TO LIFE EVENTS

For your income as a freelance interpreter, you will rely directly on your ability to log work hours. Special care and planning must be taken to handle expected and unexpected life events that could affect your ability to log hours. Any event that takes you out of work hours must be thought through.

Some examples are the following:
- Maternity/paternity
- Vacation
- Bereavement
- Sick time
- Taking care of sick family
- Auto trouble
- Medical/dental visits
- Extended medical/dental treatment or recovery

These events can seriously impact your finances if they are not thought through and planned for ahead of time!

INSURANCE

As a freelancer, you rely heavily on your ability to show up to work in order to get paid. You also are at risk for liability claims due to your personal and immediate interaction with your clients and those around them. Unexpected catastrophic risks to your income are best handled by insurance. The following are insurance areas you should consider carefully and discuss with a financial planner or insurance professional.

Disability/Dismemberment

If you suffer an illness or injury that makes you temporarily or permanently unable to serve as an interpreter, carrying this insurance can help you transition. Social Security provides for some disability coverage, but the coverage is very limited and subject to a one-year exclusion period. Short-term disability coverage typically will offer some level of wage replacement inside that year and will have a much smaller exclusion period, like 30 days. Long-term disability covers you for longer lasting or permanent disabilities.

Liability

It is important for a professional sign language interpreter to consider the impact one's interpretation can have on any given situation. This is of particular importance when interpreting in medical, mental health, and legal settings, although consideration for liability coverage should certainly **not** be limited only to those fields.

It is recommended that individuals working in these types of settings carry professional liability/errors-and-omissions insurance for their own as well as their consumers' protection. In some states, or when working with specific referral entities, liability insurance is **required** in order to perform interpretation services. Interpreters wishing to provide these services should research the laws and/or policies of their own states and referral agencies for accurate requirements.

The Registry of Interpreters for the Deaf has sponsored a liability insurance policy program that is specifically geared toward sign language interpreters. The company that underwrites such policies is Marsh. The toll-free phone number is: **1-800-503-9230** or you can send an e-mail to plssvc@seaburychicago.com **or** go to http://global.marsh.com/risk/professional/

A self-employed liability policy is available at $136.00 per year. This premium guarantees $2,000,000.00 coverage for each incident, and $4,000,000.00 for the policy aggregate. This policy is issued to individuals performing interpreting services. In order to obtain professional liability insurance sponsored by RID, an individual must be a member in good standing of RID. **It is not required that the interpreter be certified.**

There are alternate policies that agencies employing or contracting with interpreters may purchase, at a slightly higher annual premium, and with special fees for certifying "additional insureds" on policies. For more information about this, contact Marsh.

Auto

This is included only because typically, without your vehicle, you can't make it to work. You should ensure you have auto insurance adequate to replace or repair your vehicle should it be in a major accident. You should also seriously consider a rental car insurance rider, to allow you to have access to a vehicle while yours is repaired. This could make a huge difference. Imagine having to pay out of pocket for a week of car rental or losing out on a week of billable hours! If you rely on your automobile to get you to work, proper auto insurance is vital.

FIVE

Developing Yourself and Your Business

CHARACTERISTICS OF A PROFESSIONAL INTERPRETER

Successful professional sign language interpreters possess many important skills and attributes. This book does not seek to identify all possible characteristics, but to highlight those that are most critical in the eyes of the author.

One of the most critical attributes is the difficult-to-define **"attitude"** of the interpreter. An interpreter who has the right combination of professional distance, friendly approachability, respect for ASL and Deaf Culture, interpreting skills, as well as appropriate social decorum and self-monitoring/filtering, will be very successful in the interpreting profession.

Those interpreters who convey an attitude of separatism from or superiority to the Deaf consumer, display coldness or demanding behavior toward the hearing consumer, or leave their interpreter colleagues feeling less than supported will quickly find themselves without a clientele, and wondering what happened.

It is important to remember that the ability to interact skillfully within any given interpreting setting as a member of a team, while making the interpreting process as transparent as possible, is an ability that is developed over time and through repeated practice and experience. Learning how to deal with a variety of personality types is a part of the interpreting profession that is a lifelong process!

A second characteristic of a professional interpreter is **competence in American Sign Language** and the flexibility to shift along the continuum of contact language varieties to best meet the needs of each consumer. While it is clear that an interpreter must have the requisite language skills and dual tasking tools to provide interpreting services, it is important for an interpreter to gauge his or her level of comfort providing services to consumers at various ends of the sign language continuum. While one interpreter may excel at providing very deep, rich ASL interpretation, another may have a great aptitude at transliterating manually coded English. A successful interpreter will develop the insight to determine whether or not his or her skills are an appropriate match for the Deaf consumer.

One often-ignored facet of sign language interpreting is **competence in spoken English** (or the spoken language into which you are interpreting). Often, interpreters are so focused on competence in their second language (and for the majority of hearing interpreters, this is ASL) that they forget competence in English is equally important. Specifically, it is crucial to cultivate the ability to use a wide range of English vocabulary at the appropriate register[2]. In addition to vocabulary development and register match, an interpreter also must consider complex issues of how men and women use language differently. For example, how does a male Deaf consumer come across when being interpreted by a female interpreter? Is the interpreter using features of spoken language that would clearly show a male way of presenting information as opposed to that of a female? While interpreters are obviously unable to speak in the "voice" of the opposite gender, they can work towards the goal of presenting information in such a way so as to most effectively serve our consumers. For an in-depth examination of this topic, I would refer you to linguist Deborah Tannen's excellent book entitled *Talking from 9 to 5: Women and Men at Work.*

A fourth area that can create a successful professional is **competence in basic business principles** including invoicing, accounting, and basic contract development. While an interpreter does not need to become a professional accountant or tax preparer to run his or her own business, having basic skills in these areas allows an interpreter to successfully manage his or her cash flow and overall budget, while ensuring that all tax obligations are met (see Chapter Three for more information).

---

[2] Register refers to the level of formality of the language being used. Common categories of register include: frozen, formal, casual and intimate.

A final characteristic of a successful, professional interpreter is **an open mind**, and cultivating the belief that a stellar interpreter is never "done" growing and learning. No matter how many years I have been interpreting, it never ceases to amaze me the new and different things I learn every day. To believe that my capacity for knowledge and my ability to develop new skills and abilities is finite does a grave disservice to all consumers with whom I come in contact. It is **critical** that interpreters continue their quests for knowledge and skill development until the day they leave the field. Always striving to do something new, different, and challenging allows a good interpreter to become great, and an excellent interpreter to become phenomenal.

WHAT DEAF CONSUMERS CONSIDER "PROFESSIONAL"

Interpreters must always remember that without Deaf people, and their willingness to share the language of ASL with us, interpreters would not exist. We owe a debt of gratitude to all those Deaf people who were patient and willing to teach us the intricacies of their language while remaining positive and supportive and asking little, if anything, in return. While interpreting requires aptitude and a certain cognitive ability on the part of the interpreter, it is because of Deaf people's willingness to embrace our ineptitudes, and excuse our errors while allowing us to learn, that interpreting as a field exists at all. It is for all these reasons that I return to the issue of what being a "professional" really means, and how that perception differs between Deaf and hearing cultures.

In mainstream American culture, a professional is defined as: a *person who is expert at his or her work or a person who follows his or her occupation as a means of livelihood or for gain.*[3] It is interesting to note that this definition focuses primarily on the individual's ability to earn a living doing his or her job, along with possession of advanced skills warranting a professional designation. The emphasis is on individual achievement and proficiency, which parallels two strong American cultural values: individuality and success or skill.

As discussed in Mindess's book, *Reading Between the Signs,* American Deaf Culture is considered a collectivist culture, which values the goals and aims of the group above all else. No one individual's goals supersede that

---

[3] Dictionary.com Unabridged (v 1.1). Random House, Inc. 10 Oct. 2007. <Dictionary.com <Dictionary.com http://dictionary.reference.com/browse/professional>.

of the cultural group. In addition to this, success and achievement are not considered core cultural values of the Deaf community. Within Deaf Culture, while individual achievement occurs, it is not something that is emphasized or called out to other cultural members. How one is different or special is not as valued as what cultural members share in common. Values such as sharing information and reciprocity[4] are held in high regard and are core concepts at the heart of American Deaf Culture. This perspective is unfamiliar in American culture, and may be difficult for hearing interpreters to understand and/or mediate.

So what does a Deaf person perceive as "professional"? The answer to this will vary among Deaf consumers, but overall, an interpreter with competent skills and a positive, empowering attitude will go far in the field. It is important to remember that Deaf and hearing people value different qualities as being professional. Understanding this and cultivating a balance will allow an interpreter to be successful in both hearing and Deaf cultures.

CONTINUING EDUCATION: THE NECESSITY OF A MENTOR

Often, business books will recommend finding a mentor in your chosen field. This book is no different. Mentors are seasoned professionals who have the ability to help you develop your existing skills, and who provide feedback for growing and improving as a professional. I cannot stress enough the importance of finding a mentor (or mentors) early on in your interpreting career.

It is important that you attempt to seek out someone to mentor you who has the following skills, characteristics and abilities:

- Extensive knowledge of the interpreting field

- Ability to provide meaningful and constructive feedback

- Willingness to answer questions and have insightful discussions

- The respect of those within the field of interpreting and in the Deaf Community

---

[4] Reciprocity is defined as giving to and taking from the collective skills in the group, which is often a feature of collectivist culture.

- Belief that lifelong learning is the cornerstone of being a professional interpreter

- Commitment to giving back to the field by encouraging and helping to grow new as well as seasoned interpreters

There are several questions you should ask yourself when selecting a mentor. The following list will help guide you toward choosing someone who can best help you achieve your professional goals.

1. What is the goal toward which I am working and on which I wish to focus at this time? (e.g., I want to incorporate more classifier use in my expressive interpreting.)

2. Whom can I enlist that might be willing/able to provide me with mentorship in this area?

3. How do I want to request and receive feedback?

4. Whom do I feel I can trust with my areas of weakness?

5. What kinds of activities could provide my mentor with opportunities to give me feedback?

6. How will I know I have made satisfactory progress towards achieving my goal? (How is success measured?)

7. How much time and effort will this require?

8. Am I willing to compensate my mentor for his or her time, and if so, how much?

Once you have answered these questions, you will be equipped to approach your potential mentor and ask him or her to provide mentorship, while specifying parameters such as what kind of feedback you are seeking and how your progress will be measured.

Having a concrete goal and ideas about how to achieve it will help your mentor understand how to best serve you, and will allow you the maximum benefit from the mentorship. It is very difficult for a mentor to provide assistance if the mentee has nebulous goals with little or no idea how to achieve them.

A thoughtful approach to skill development will go far in allowing you to communicate with your mentor and ultimately achieve your goals.

After you have mentally selected potential mentors and answered the questions above, it is time to formulate a plan of action. Write up a short, one-page proposal of what your mentorship needs are, and approach your mentor candidates to see if they are interested. The proposal might look something like this:

Proposal for Mentorship Services
Name: Interpreter A
Potential Mentor: Interpreter B/Deaf Person A
Goal for Improvement: Increased incorporation and appropriate use of classifiers in expressive interpretation.
Method of Feedback: In-person 1:1 discussion about videotaped interpretation segments, and/or debriefing after working together in a team interpreting session. Pre- and post-mentorship quantitative analysis of classifier use.
Time Requirement: 1 hour per week for 6 weeks (mentor-mentee discussions, review of videotapes)
Compensation of Mentor: $45 per week x 6 weeks = $270.00
Possible Activities:
1. Mentee will videotape him/herself interpreting a pre-recorded text at the beginning of the mentorship. This text should have sufficient content that would require the use of classifiers in ASL.

2. Mentee will discuss with mentor areas of improvement based on feedback from viewing the initial recorded text. Mentor will suggest strategies for incorporation of classifiers into the mentee's interpretation.

3. Mentor and mentee will continue to work on various texts and/or debrief real-time interpreting situations with the classifier goal in mind.

4. After mentorship period has concluded, mentee will re-interpret the initial pre-recorded text in order to determine improvements in classifier use over the term of the mentorship.

5. Mentor will compare initial and final video recordings of mentee to ascertain areas of improvement still needed, and goals achieved.

Potential Start Date: _____ **Potential End Date:** _____

It is not always necessary to have a formal mentorship agreement; however, it can often make the process clearer and the expectations for both mentor and mentee more concrete. Regardless of the formality of the agreement, having a trusted mentor is a critical component of lifelong learning and commitment to professional development.

Many interpreters fall into the trap of believing that simply collecting Continuing Education Units (CEUs) needed to maintain certification is a sufficient way to continue to grow as a professional. While attending professional development activities is encouraged and required, it is not the only way to build skills and improve abilities.

GETTING YOUR FOOT IN THE DOOR: HOW TO FIND WORK

Like many service professions, sign language interpreting is largely a word-of-mouth business. A competent interpreter with an excellent attitude will often become known through colleague and/or consumer referral. However, it is necessary to get out into the working world in order to become a known quantity and consequently get referred. Depending on your level of experience and areas of comfort, there are many places you might contact in order to obtain work. The following is a list of entities potentially needing interpreting services:

1. Post-secondary educational institutions (colleges, universities, community colleges, professional/technical programs)

2. Video relay services

3. Sign language interpreter referral services

   a. Private, for-profit agencies

   b. Non-profit agencies

   c. State-run commissions for the deaf and hard of hearing

4. K-12 public education system

5. Foreign language interpreter referral services

6. State and local government agencies

While this list is by no means exhaustive, and various companies, agencies, and entities may not be listed here, the majority of an interpreter's work is obtained through association with interpreter referral agencies. Usually, this means that rather than contracting with an individual interpreter, a service requester (such as a hospital) will contract with a referral service to fill its interpreting service needs. This is more cost effective for an entity that makes multiple requests, because the interpreter referral agency is a centralized clearinghouse that deals with each individual interpreter's invoices, and then sends one comprehensive invoice for services to the service requester each month. There are many ways to locate entities with which to contract for services. Here are some of the best ones:

1. Contact local interpreter training programs and ask for a current list of interpreter referral agencies, K-12 educational interpreter coordinators in the local area, state commissions for the deaf and hard of hearing contact people, names of recruiters and local video relay service centers, names of local colleges and universities providing interpreting services, and the names of their access coordinators.

2. Ask for similar referrals from established, local professional interpreters who know the area and can recommend trusted agencies with whom to contract.

3. Google local colleges and universities to locate access coordinator contact information. Use search terms such as Disability Resource Center, ADA Coordinator, Access Coordinator, Disabled Student Services, Accommodations, or Sign Language Interpreting Services.

4. Create an introduction package that allows coordinators to see your skills and qualifications. Include in the package:

    •   A current resume

    •   Copies of your certification(s), if any

- Copy of your liability insurance policy

- 1-2 letters of reference (especially from locally respected professionals and/or Deaf consumers)

- A cover letter indicating your interest in freelance interpreting work (or full-time employment if this is your goal)

- A copy of your current Terms of Services Agreement (TOSA) (see Chapter Seven)

- A current business card

Make a list of entities to which you would like to send your introductory packet. Try to send these packets to specific individuals who have the authority to hire you to provide services. Avoid sending materials to non-specific entities such as "Human Resources," "Personnel Department," or "Access Coordinator." The person who could hire you will likely never see such vague submissions.

Be specific in your letter. Include information about who referred you to the agency/coordinator/entity, and why you would be a good match for the clientele this entity serves. Ask for a follow-up call, or indicate in your letter that you will be calling to set up a time to meet and discuss potential job opportunities. Include a valid means of contact (e.g., phone numbers and e-mail addresses) so the service requester can respond to your request.

Follow through! After one to two weeks, if you have not heard from the contact people, call or e-mail them so that you can gauge the job opportunities available. **ASK QUESTIONS!!**

1. What kinds of job opportunities are available?

2. Does the entity contract individually with interpreters, or through a referral agency, or hire staff people?

3. What kinds of rates is the entity used to paying? *[5]

---

[5] All questions marked with * can be omitted if the entity to which you are applying simply agrees to the terms you present in your terms of services agreement. These issues should all be addressed within your document.

4. How does the entity handle situations that may require a team of interpreters (e.g., assignments over 1.5 hours)? *

5. Is there anyone currently providing interpreting services to the entity that you might be able to contact in order to get a reference about the entity?

6. Does the entity require any special qualifications, pre-employment requirements, or background checks to be performed before hiring?

7. Are interpreters required to display any specific badges or forms of identification when providing interpreting services?

8. What is the entity's cancellation policy? *

Another excellent way to develop individual contracts is to establish a website that provides the community with a way to locate your services. Almost no interpreting business is generated by a listing in the Yellow Pages; however, many potential service requesters have located my services via searching for local "sign language interpreters" on the Internet. Websites are generally very inexpensive to have hosted, and there are a multitude of site builders that will allow you to design your own site without being knowledgeable in computer coding. Websites are also excellent ways of providing frequently requested information to people, such as information on the Americans with Disabilities Act (ADA), your resume and/or terms of services agreement, current copies of the Registry of Interpreters for the Deaf (RID) Standards and Practices Papers, etc.

There are literally limitless types and styles of websites from which you can choose, but there are a few things that you should keep in mind when designing your site.

1. Make the design clean and professional with easy navigation.

2. Use visually accessible colors and fonts that are not harsh on the eyes, and are easy to read.

3. Include links to the following pieces of information for your site visitors:

- Your current resume[6]

- Video samples of your interpreting work

- Your current terms of services agreement '

- List of links to helpful or related sites

- Applicable interpreting or access provision-related documents (e.g., RID Standards and Practices Papers, ADA information)

4. Keep your website up to date. Make sure that links are still working and all information is current.

For an example of one way to highlight your services on a website, visit my website at: http://www.nwasla.com

TEAM INTERPRETING[7]

While it may seem an odd placement for this section, I believe that team interpreting is one of the most effective ways to develop oneself as an interpreter. Not only does team interpreting afford you the opportunity to develop relationships with colleagues, it also is a rich environment in which to learn new ways to convey information, and to refine your interpreting process.

It is extremely important to develop a positive perspective on team interpretation. Team interpretation not only increases the overall accuracy of message transmission, but also allows us as practitioners to continue to enhance our skills and help one another grow. While many interpreters have had the experience of feeling as if team interpreting is a competition between the two team members, it is critical to remember that the goal of an effective team is overall message accuracy as well as professional service provision, rather than one-upmanship.

Team interpreting has grown and changed over the last 40 years. Originally, team interpreters were viewed as two interpreters who "spelled" each other in 15-20 minute increments and were only placed in job assignments that were

---

[6] See the Appendix for samples of a management as well as an interpreting resume.

[7] See the Team Interpreting Sample Form in the Appendix for questions to ask when attempting to determine whether or not a team interpreter is required.

two hours or more in length. The reason for this was the idea that the need for a team of interpreters was due to the physical fatigue and overuse injuries that were occurring for interpreters working alone for longer than two hours at a time. During the team interpretation process, one interpreter would serve as the "on" interpreter working to provide services to the Deaf consumer, while the other interpreter would quite literally be "off" and often leave the room to take a break, make phone calls, or take a brief walk. There was really little in the way of teamwork occurring other than to determine at what time interval the interpreters wanted to switch positions.

There are numerous reasons why this method was/is less than effective. First, a team of interpreters working in this fashion are not providing support to one another in order to enhance message accuracy. No feeds are being given, and missed information is not being provided to the "on" interpreter by the "off" interpreter. Secondly, if one interpreter leaves the room for any length of time, he or she then misses the content of what is being said during his or her absence, and lacks context when it is his or her turn to take over the interpreting task. It is also difficult to maintain a consistent communication style between interpreters, which in turn can make it difficult for the Deaf consumer to watch. Next, if specialized signs or vocabulary are negotiated between the Deaf consumer and "on" interpreter, the "off" interpreter misses these negotiations, and often ends up re-negotiating or having to catch up on what has already been established because he or she was not present. Finally, there is a sense of disconnection and distance from the process and from the Deaf consumer when team interpreting is done in this way. This type of practice does not lend itself to collegiality, enhanced learning, mentorship or full and complete, seamless interpretation.

As the field of interpreting has grown and progressed, and interpreters have become more aware of the real rationale for team interpreting, the practice has changed greatly. In addition to the idea that interpreters become physically fatigued after a given period of time (usually around 60 minutes), it has been widely shown that an interpreter's mental processing and accuracy starts to suffer far earlier than this (at about 15-20 minutes depending on content complexity). The issue of declining accuracy, while always something interpreters wish to avoid, has become even more critical in settings such as mental health, medical, and legal, where Deaf consumers' lives may be at stake.

One of the two variations of team interpreting currently in use has the following components:

1. Both interpreters remain present in the interpreting setting at all times (with the exception of scheduled breaks, bathroom needs, etc.). The team discusses with one another how switches of interpreters will take place, at what time interval, and how each team member will give and receive feeds. Interpreters are generally seated in such a way that the "on" and "off" interpreters are facing one another in order to give and receive feeds.

2. The "on" interpreter solicits, receives, and incorporates feeds from his or her team member.

3. The team of interpreters communicates via a notepad kept at the "off" interpreter's seat.

4. The "off" interpreter takes responsibility for all logistical adjustments needed during the "on" interpreter's work session (e.g., adjustment of lighting, sound, access to visual information, checking to see if things are Closed Captioned, etc.).

5. The team of interpreters works together to negotiate specialized signs with the Deaf consumer.

6. If the team is working in a specialized setting, such as a legal setting, the team will discuss how witness testimony will be handled, team interpreter positioning, and consecutive interpreting support strategies.

7. If time permits, the team debriefs about the assignment at its conclusion.

In this traditional approach to team interpreting, the "off" or "feed" interpreter often sits outside of a Deaf person's peripheral view, and the active interpreter must re-create the "off" partner's "feeds" in the interpretation. Interpreting issues and problem solving are handled by the interpreting team, and generally do not include the Deaf participant's input. This could be viewed as a **"closed" process.**

While this traditional method of team interpreting is very effective and has been in use at various levels for a number of years, an even more novel approach has come about in the last few years, and is known as the **Open Process Model** of team interpreting.

The open process model of interpreting was conceived by RID certified interpreters Molly Wilson and Vivian Berry of New York State, and then further developed and taught by Ms. Wilson. Molly, a native signer from a multi-generation Deaf family, first introduced the model at Allies Conferences in New Hampshire. This model has been in existence for some time and has been used largely on the East Coast. It is now making its way to the West Coast interpreting and Deaf communities through workshops and community forums developed, taught, and hosted by Ms. Wilson.

The Open Process Model is designed to literally "open" the team interpreting process to Deaf participants, inviting full participation in the traditionally closed interpreting process. Interpreters working in an open process will usually sit side-by-side rather than across from one another. Use of natural ASL discourse allows team members to step in and out of the flow of their partner's interpretation as needed. Both interpreters are actively processing the information, and if Interpreter A misses a concept or needs help in conveying it to the Deaf participant, Interpreter B is right there to briefly step into the interpretation. The ability to maintain message integrity is increased because, using the same visual perspective, interpreters can share and manipulate the same signing space when correcting, clarifying or turn taking. Because the entire process happens in full view of the Deaf participant, that individual, too, has the option of stepping into the interpretation for clarification or correction at any time.

While this approach is seen as quite a divergence from traditional team interpreting, the benefits for all parties involved in the communication event can be tremendous. Not only does the Deaf participant have the opportunity to be a complete part of the process and enhance his or her ability to understand the information being presented, but also the interpreters are able to actively work together to make communication as seamless and culturally relevant as possible.

SIX

The Ethics of Choosing an Agency

FREELANCE INTERPRETERS HAVE a number of options when deciding on a home base from which to access their assignments. One of the many options is to work for an interpreter referral agency either as a staff interpreter or as an independent contractor. Choosing which agency(ies) to work with, if any, however, is something an interpreter should consider carefully.

Generally, agencies that refer sign language interpreters fall into three different categories:

- Sign-language **only** interpreter referral agencies; either for-profit or non-profit (e.g., state-run commissions for the deaf and hard of hearing).
- Foreign language referral agencies that also refer sign language interpreters
- Temporary service agencies (like Kelly Services) that contract all vendor services for large companies (e.g., Microsoft, Hewlett Packard).

This chapter will talk about the issues freelance interpreters should take into consideration before deciding whether or not to work through an agency, and/or which agency(ies) to choose.

TYPES OF REFERRAL AGENCIES

Sign Language Only Referral Agencies

These agencies specialize in sign language and other types of interpretation and transliteration specific to Deaf and hard-of-hearing individuals. These agencies may provide Deaf interpreters as well. Sign-language-only agencies provide **only** sign language interpreters, and do not provide foreign language interpreters (although they may provide foreign sign language interpreters). In general, these types of agencies have specialized knowledge and expertise specific to the needs of Deaf and hard-of-hearing consumers, and providers of sign language interpretation services. These agencies are well-versed in the requirements of sign language interpretation such as team interpreting and the use of Certified Deaf Interpreters (CDIs).

In some metropolitan areas with large Deaf and hard-of-hearing populations, sign-language-only agencies may offer both staff interpreter positions and contract positions depending on the volume of requests the agency handles. Some agencies that are large enough to employ staff interpreters provide benefits such as health insurance, vacation time, and professional development. It is important for an interpreter to determine what type of position he/she wishes to undertake. It is also critical that interpreters understand the tax implications of providing services as an employee versus as an independent contractor, and how these two statuses differ.

Traditionally, sign language interpreters, Deaf professionals, or other individuals with education or special knowledge of interpretation, business, and deafness have established sign language interpreter referral agencies. Often, these agencies attempt to hire interpreter coordinators who have knowledge and training in matching client preference and linguistic needs to interpreter qualifications. Another successful combination is an office manager who is an excellent businessperson and coordinator, and who works closely with professional interpreting staff members who are well versed in assessment of interpreter skill levels and qualifications.

Foreign Language Referral Agencies

These usually are larger agencies that focus on providing interpretation and/or translation of a broad range of foreign languages and dialects to a variety of entities. Often, when competing for language contracts, they will be asked to provide a bid for all-in-one interpreting services, which includes sign language. This can be problematic for foreign language agencies with no experience working with sign language interpreters, or for those agencies that commit to providing sign language interpretation. There is a basic lack of understanding of sign language interpreting as a field, as well as of the terms and expectations under which sign language interpreters provide services.

Foreign language agencies can be very large and well reputed (e.g., Berlitz), or smaller and less formally run. Some agencies provide only telephone interpretation or document translation, while others provide call-out services. This book contains no information on how or if these agencies determine the qualifications of their interpreters. Agencies could simply refer individuals who claim they are competent interpreters but in reality may not be. This is sometimes called the "warm body" appointment-filling theory. Most foreign language agencies that are new to working with sign language interpreters are usually surprised at the marked price differences among different types of interpreters. Positions for sign language interpreters at these agencies are generally independent contractor opportunities.

Temporary Service Agencies

Many large corporations, such as Microsoft Corporation and Hewlett Packard, require **all** of their contracted or vendor services be handled through a central temporary service agency. In these cases, sign language interpreters would be required to become **employees** of the temporary service (which means that all applicable income tax and other withholdings would be deducted from the interpreters' paychecks). Working with these agencies requires compliance agreements that often are unlike those found in agencies focused on sign language, such as: confidential disclosure agreements, submission to a drug test and background check, agreement on rate of pay, hourly minimums, and mileage payment.

Many interpreters grumble about this type of arrangement; however, it definitely has its pros! For example, in some cases, if an interpreter is an employee of a temporary service and works more than 20-30 hours per week, he/she is eligible for benefits just as any other worker would be. Some temporary services pay for professional development opportunities such as taking additional certification exams or attending workshops to improve one's skills. Many temporary services are willing to pay interpreters the going rate and appropriate minimums, as well as continuing to provide team interpreters as per the industry standard. The main difference is tax withholdings from the interpreter's paycheck. The best part is direct deposit of your paycheck into your checking account every Friday without fail!

A key point with temporary services is to realize that the interpreter coordinator may or may not have experience working with sign language. That person may not have the knowledge or ability to determine the language needs of Deaf people, or be able to assess an assignment to accurately decide on the number of interpreters needed. It is critical to recognize this limitation and work with the coordinator in a positive way to educate and to enhance the situation.

CHOOSING AN AGENCY – THE PROCESS

Now that we have discussed the various types of agencies, how do you decide where you want to work? Should you sign up with everyone and see what happens? Should you put all your money on one horse and hope for a win? Should you forgo agency work altogether and try contracting with individual companies on your own? All of these ideas are viable options, and the rest of this chapter will give you the tools you need to make your decision.

Interview the Agencies

Remember, these agencies are earning money from the excellent work and professional services you provide. **Without you, they would have no business.** It is important that your goals and values are in line with those of the agency you represent and that sells your services. When deciding if you are interested in linking yourself and your reputation with an agency, always keep in mind that the most important things you have as a professional are your ethics, integrity, and skills.

These are some of the key questions that an interpreter should ask when speaking with an agency and deciding if working with that agency is a good fit:

- Inquire about the background of the agency owner and/or interpreter coordinator(s). Sometimes one person serves in both roles and sometimes the tasks are divided among a number of people. Find out if those who contract and hire interpreters have backgrounds in assessment of sign language interpreters or are aware of the various skill requirements, training, and/or education that competent interpreters should have.
- Ask if the agency has a written policy and procedure manual that outlines information such as billing policies (e.g., what dates paychecks

are mailed, if there is a specific date that invoices are due each month, if the agency requires that vouchers or other confirmation documents be signed at job sites, etc.).

- Find out what kind of hourly rates the agency is used to paying for various services. Are there differentials for evening, legal, on-call, tactile, or performance assignments? In what increments are services billed: 1-hour, ½-hour, or ¼-hour increments? Are there any service minimums?
- Inquire as to policies regarding team interpretation.
- Find out whether or not travel time and/or mileage are compensated. Get specifics.
- Inquire about the agency's cancellation policy for assignments, and at what rate the agency is used to paying. Does the policy vary depending on assignment length (e.g., 24 hours' notice for any assignment 1-3 hours in length, 48 hours' notice for any assignment 4-8 hours in length), or is it a flat policy regardless of assignment length?
- Does the agency use or support the use of Deaf interpreters?
- Does the agency charge a referral fee to the interpreter being referred work (e.g., if the fee is 5% of each hour of interpreting work referred, and the pay rate is 1 hour at $40.00, the interpreter will receive $38.00 and the agency will receive $2.00)? Keep in mind that the referral agency is also charging the hearing service requester a referral fee.
- Ask the agency if it could provide you with the names of other interpreters with whom it has contracted. Take the time to ask those interpreters about their experiences working with that agency.
- Ask the agency if it honors Deaf consumer preference/non-preference with regard to interpreter choice.
- Ask the agency if the state requires any state interpreter Quality Assurance (QA) certification and/or licensure, and if so, what is it?
- Ask the agency if it has a grievance policy for consumers of its services as well as for interpreters.

Speak with Reputable Professionals in the Area

If you have relocated recently, or you are just getting started as a freelancer, it is good advice to speak with certified interpreters in the local area who are well-established and can give you candid feedback about the agencies in a given region. Those who have been involved in the field of interpreting for a number of years will be able to report patterns and changes with both foreign language and sign language referral agencies. All interpreters have their biases, but some good information can be found by speaking with:

- Interpreter trainers at accredited interpreter training/preparation programs
- Certified interpreters
- State and local commissions for the deaf and hard of hearing
- Personal referrals by respected professionals (working interpreters/ Deaf consumers)

Once you have found references to check, what kinds of questions should you ask? The most important thing to remember is that, when working in a reciprocal relationship, both parties must benefit in order for the relationship to work. When speaking with the references, find out how the relationship has been working for them. Some sample questions might look like:

1. Does the agency you work for consistently pay you in a timely fashion as per your written agreement with them, and as per the rate(s) agreed upon?
2. Does the agency provide you adequate, **correct** information in advance about the job assignments you accept, including client, location, job context, job numbers and other information?
3. Does the agency consistently and appropriately assess the need for team interpreters and provide them; and if you request a team interpreter does the agency advocate for and get that team interpreter for you?
4. Does the agency provide you with team interpreters of sufficient skill level to work effectively in a team environment?
5. Does the agency respond proactively or dismissively to the feedback you give?
6. Does the agency honor Deaf consumer preference/non-preference with regard to choice of interpreter(s)?
7. What has your experience been, overall, with this agency?

Make Your Decision

Now that you have done your research, it is time to make your decision. But before you start presenting your proposal to various agencies, let's take a look at some things that should **definitely** make you stop and think before you sign up.

➡ **Unfavorable record with the Better Business Bureau:** Not all businesses are registered with the BBB, but they don't have to be for someone to contact the Bureau and register a complaint about a business. These complaints stay on record, and you can call the Bureau and inquire as to whether or not any complaints have been registered against an agency. States have varying laws regarding the confidentiality of the contents of such complaints. This means you may or may not be able to find out the substance of the complaint.

➡ **Non-sufficient funds (NSF) Checks:** If any of the references with whom you have spoken has reported receiving an NSF check – RUN. It is likely to happen again and more than once. If you are the gambling sort, hey, go for it, but I wouldn't recommend it.

➡ **The phrase, "We can't pay you until we get paid,"** Guess what? When you have a contract with an agency, you have exactly that: a contract with **the agency** – not the hospital or business paying the agency. That is the whole point of going through the agency and not just working for the hospital or business yourself. So, this means if the interpreter and the agency have a contract that says the interpreter will be paid no later than 15 or 30 days from the date of invoice, then that is when the agency **must** pay the interpreter or the agency is in breach of contract. It makes no difference if the hospital or business hasn't paid the agency yet. It is the agency's responsibility to come up with the money to pay the interpreter for services rendered. If an agency asks you to work under this policy, which I affectionately call, "We'll pay you when we get around to it," politely decline.

➡ **Gross underpayment:** In order to snap up large contracts, some agencies will underbid all others by quoting extremely low rates, often beneath industry standard. Interpreters are then expected to work for peanuts in order to maintain the contract for the agency. This not only undermines interpreters' attempts to secure appropriate wages for services provided, but also creates unrealistic expectations on the parts of service requestors when trying to budget for interpreting services. Most importantly, Deaf consumers are the ones most impacted because few interpreters are willing to work under poor conditions. Watch for agencies that engage in this practice

➡ **Questionable suggestions:** If an agency ever suggests to you that rather than paying you (as agreed) for an assignment, you can just write off the amount billed for the assignment on your taxes as a tax deduction, alarm bells should be ringing. Not only is this not accurate (bad debt write-offs have very specific restrictions – consult your tax professional), but it is a breach of contract. One party cannot change the terms of a contract without the consent of the other party.

Submit Your Proposal

Once you have decided the agencies with which you are interested in working, contact the interpreter coordinator or hiring manager, and either submit an application (if you are applying for full-time work) or make an appointment to discuss a proposal for contract work. At this meeting you should bring the following items with you:

1. Two (or more) written copies of your contract proposal (including proposed terms regarding hourly rate, differentials, cancellation policies, team interpretation policies, terms of payment, applicable late fees, policies regarding referral charges (if any), information regarding hourly minimums, travel time, mileage, and/or policies regarding videotaping of work product, etc.).
2. Several business cards
3. Copies of your interpreter certification(s)
4. Copy of your liability insurance certificate
5. Copy of your resume
6. Copies of any letters of recommendation
7. Copies of any videos/DVDs of signing samples you may wish to provide, or that have been requested by the agency.

During the meeting, discuss the terms and conditions under which you wish to provide services, and under which the agency is able to offer you contract work. Be willing to be flexible, but not so flexible as to agree to terms with which you aren't comfortable. No matter what: **get everything in writing.** Finally, have a copy of the final agreement signed by the hiring manager or authorized agent and yourself before beginning to provide services. Both you and the agency should each retain a copy of the agreement to refer to should any questions arise as to the terms of service provision.

One of the most important concepts that an interpreter needs to understand is that if he or she agrees to work for an agency, and that agency engages in unscrupulous business practices or undermines the standards set by practicing members of the sign language interpreting profession, that interpreter is tacitly supporting these practices by continuing to work at the agency.

One of the most common concerns that I have heard expressed by freelance interpreters is, "If I quit working for (insert agency name here), then I will be blackballed or I won't have any work." My response to this is, "If you are a skilled interpreter with an excellent attitude and a high level of integrity, you will be able to find sufficient work." In addition to this, if more interpreters stood their ground and refused to work for unscrupulous agencies, these agencies would cease to exist because they would have no referral pool from which to draw.

Finally, thinking logically, if an interpreter is not being paid by an agency, or is constantly being paid late, and yet he or she continues to accept work from that agency, how is this any different from not working for the agency at all? In either case (whether the interpreter does not accept work or whether the interpreter accepts work but does not get paid), the interpreter is still providing services for free. Who loses? The interpreter does. This is not an attempt to discount the value of pro bono (at no charge) services. However, those types of services should be agreed upon in advance. Only by refusing to be taken advantage of and by maintaining high personal integrity as professionals can interpreters help advance the profession while weeding out predatory businesses.

SEVEN

The Written Contract: Don't Leave Home Without It!

IF YOU LEARN NOTHING else from this book, take to heart the information in this chapter. To me, it is the single most important business-related part of your professional development. The simple take-away point from this chapter is: **unless you are willing to perform the service for free, NEVER provide services without a written contract in place prior to service provision.**

A contract is a legally binding exchange of promises or an agreement between parties that the law will enforce. In common law, there are three key elements to the creation of a contract: offer and acceptance, consideration, and an intention to create a legal relationship. [8]

It is critical that you recognize the significance of the written contract and what it means to you as a business professional providing services. The offer and acceptance of a contract is viewed in the eyes of the law as a meeting of the minds. It is this meeting of the minds that is important when establishing terms and conditions under which you are to provide services. If there is a dispute about payment later, it is much easier to refer to the written contract each party agreed to, rather than trying to enforce a verbal "handshake" type of agreement.

CONTRACT COMPONENTS

An effective written contract can be as general or specific as you like; however, at a minimum, the following components should be included:

- **Statement of work:** This is a brief summary statement of the services that are to be supplied under your contract.

---

[8] http://en.wikipedia.org/wiki/Contract

- **Consideration for services:** Consideration is the basis of a contract. This is the specified rate that you will be charging for a given service. Your section on consideration can include a breakdown of rates charged for different times of day or types of assignments. This section should also include any reimbursement for travel time, mileage, per diem, lodging, and transportation if applicable.

- **Cancellation Policy:** Your cancellation policy should outline the time by which a service requester must cancel your services in order not to incur charges. Generally, it is a good idea to break down the cancellation policy based on the length of the job assignment (e.g., the longer the job assignment, the further in advance the service requester must cancel in order not to incur a fee).

- **Payment Terms:** Your payment terms should be indicated so the service requester knows how quickly you require payment. Usually, independent contractors are paid on a net 30 basis, which means payment within 30 days of date of invoice. However, this is not set in stone. You can often set payment terms that are shorter in length, such as net 15 or upon receipt.

- **Signature lines** for both contractor and service requester indicating agreement to the terms.

These items comprise what I like to call my Terms of Services Agreement (TOSA). An example of a TOSA is included at the conclusion of this chapter for reference. While this is the format I have found to be most effective, it is by no means the only one. The information included in the sample agreement is comprehensive to encompass the varied types of interpreting services I provide. You can tailor the agreement to work for you.

When I emphasize the need for a written contract, interpreters often say they have never used one, and have had no trouble getting paid. They wonder why I am so insistent on this particular point. Some people believe that because they are new to the field, requiring a written contract is presumptuous of them, and might be mistaken for arrogance. While I would like to believe that everyone who makes use of my services understands and is willing to compensate me for them, this is sadly not the case. As an independent contractor, I can't afford to wait for months to be paid, or not to be paid at all. All it takes is non-payment of one lengthy assignment adding up to a large dollar amount to completely devastate your cash flow and leave you wishing for some recourse.

If you are a practitioner who has traditionally worked without a contract and **not** had trouble getting paid, I say you are lucky. If you are a practitioner who has been burned, don't let it happen twice. It is **standard business practice** for professional services to require a written contract. Businesses are rarely surprised by a request to sign a TOSA or have contractual terms agreed upon in advance. There is nothing that frustrates me more than to encounter a colleague who provides services to someone, doesn't get paid, and then continues to work without a contract. It is simply a bad business practice. Moreover, once you work for an entity and do not get paid, **don't** continue to work for the offending agency. Interpreters who continue to work for disreputable agencies that refuse to pay them consistently are allowing those agencies to exploit them and ultimately undermine the entire profession. I have actually had practitioners excuse such behavior by saying that they don't want to be "blackballed" by an agency or lose work if they refuse to provide services after not having been paid. To this I say, which is smarter, not to work at all, or to work, and not get paid? Ultimately the result is the same—**you don't get paid.** However, you can bet that the agency is still getting its referral fee. Don't get taken advantage of!

The three methods I have found most effective for transmitting TOSAs to potential service requesters are via e-mail attachment, fax, or as downloadable files from my website. These are quick ways to get information to and from the service requester, and electronic acceptance of terms via e-mail is as binding as a handwritten signature. This also takes care of the need for timely transmission of terms prior to accepting a last minute assignment.

It is not necessary that you resend your TOSA every time you interpret at a repeat location. However, it is recommended that it be sent to any entity that is a first-time client, and especially to any entity that is offering you extensive hours of work.

COLLECTION OF PAST DUE ACCOUNTS

Unfortunately, as independent business entities, sometimes interpreters have to chase down payments for services rendered. Sometimes invoices are put off for months. Professional interpreters can adopt the same protocol that other professional entities do when collecting monies due. The following is a guided tour explaining the proper process for collecting on an invoice.

1. Once the agreed upon net date for payment (e.g., 30 days) has passed, allow a 2-day grace period to account for weekends or possible holidays.

2. If the check is still not received once the grace period has passed, call the entity and ask to speak with accounts payable. Inquire as to where the invoice is in the billing process: "Hi, my name is_____, and I am calling regarding an invoice for sign language interpreting services. The invoice number is_____, and the date of the invoice was_____. The amount was_____. Currently, this payment is past due, and I wondered when I might expect to receive it?"

   NOTE: **During any payment discussions/interactions, make sure to take down the name(s) of the individuals with whom you spoke, the date, the time, and the content of the conversation, especially the date given as to when a check will be received.**

3. If the check is not received either by the date expected, or 7-10 days after it was due (whichever comes first), send a second billing with an accruing late charge marked **"Past Due."** Along with this billing, send a letter recapping the situation including the conversation with accounts payable, and the time frame that was quoted for receipt of the check. Set a deadline for receipt of payment and indicate that the next step will be collections.

   Sample letter:

   To Whom It May Concern:
   I provided sign language interpreting services on [date]. My invoice, number_____, dated_____, in the amount of _____, was due on_____. On [date], 20__, I contacted the accounts payable department and spoke with

_____ at [time]. He/She assured me that payment would be remitted by [date]. To date, I have not received payment for services rendered.

Enclosed, please find a second invoice with a late charge of $_____. If I do not receive payment by [date], I will be forced to turn this matter over to collections.

Thank you for your time and prompt attention to this matter.

Sincerely,
[name]

4. If payment has not been remitted by the deadline in your letter, submit a third invoice with what is known as a formal demand letter. Sample demand letters can be found all over the Internet by searching the terms "demand for payment letters."

5. If payment is **still** not remitted by the deadline, consider submitting the bill to a collections agency or taking the entity to small claims court. For more information on options, contact a reputable attorney with experience in contract law or employment law.

SAMPLE TOSA[9]

TERMS OF SERVICES AGREEMENT

SCOPE OF WORK: This document constitutes the terms of services agreement for provision of sign language interpreting services by Tammera J. Richards, BS, CI and CT; SC:L; NAD IV, certified sign language interpreter.

RATES OF PAY: Unless otherwise negotiated in advance, the regular daily rate of payment from 8 AM-5 PM M-F will consist of a $100.00 initial fee and then $50.00 per hour billable in 1/2 hour increments thereafter.

Unless otherwise negotiated in advance, the after hours' 5 PM-8 AM M-F and 24 hours' rate Saturday and Sunday will consist of a $110.00 initial fee and then $55.00 per hour billable in 1/2 hour increments thereafter.

---

[9] See template of a basic TOSA you can use to create your own in the Sample Forms section.

Unless otherwise negotiated in advance, legal interpreting assignments will consist of a $120.00 initial fee and then $60.00 per hour billable in 1/2-hour increments thereafter. ANY legal assignments, regardless of length, that will include deaf witness testimony will require a team interpreter to ensure accuracy of the record.

TEAM INTERPRETING POLICY: A team interpreter will be provided for any job assignment that is over 1.5 hours unless otherwise negotiated in advance. The interpreter reserves the right to negotiate a team interpreter for assignments less than 1.5 hours in length should an individual job warrant a team. Should a team of two interpreters have been expected and/or warranted and is not provided, contractor reserves the right to either charge double for work performed or work half the scheduled time without the requisite team in order to prevent injury from occurring, whichever works best to the benefit of both contracting parties.

PERFORMING ARTS ASSIGNMENTS: Performing Arts assignments will be negotiated on a per assignment, flat rate basis and will NOT be subject to regular hourly rates. All performing arts assignments will be teamed, and will require no less than two weeks of rehearsal unless otherwise negotiated—the preferred notice is 30 days or more for performance assignments.

TRAVEL TIME: Travel that is more than 1 hour in length round-trip will be billed at 1/2 the interpreter's hourly rate per hour of travel unless otherwise negotiated.

MINIMUMS: For those entities that are out of the local service area (a 40-mile round trip from my home) and/or have rate caps that are less than my hourly rate, or do not allow travel time to be billed will be subject to an initial fee of $150.00 for services.

VIDEO RECORDING AND USE OF WORK PRODUCT: All requests for video recording of interpretation work product performed by Tammera J. Richards must be contracted for in advance of the work assignment. In general, video recording of work product will be acceptable IF the following conditions are met:

- Tammera J. Richards is provided an unedited copy of the entire video recorded work product within 15 days of the date of service for her records and future use.
- The entity video recording the likeness of Tammera J. Richards will in no way profit from the use or reuse of the videotape/DVD made of the work product in the future.
- The videotape/DVD will not be used for any illicit or illegal purposes in the future.

Should these conditions not be met, video recording of work product will not be permitted, or will incur an additional fee no less than $500.00 for the initial recording, and $500.00 per showing after the initial event.

CANCELLATION POLICY: Unless otherwise negotiated in advance, required notice for cancellation of interpretation services are as follows:

ASSIGNMENT LENGTH:
1-2 hours   48 weekday hours' notice.
3-5 hours   72 weekday hours' notice.
6-8 hours   96 weekday hours' notice.

Cancellation policy for multiple day assignments will be negotiated on a per assignment basis. Weekday hours are defined as 24 hours Monday through Friday. Should cancellation of assignment not fall within these deadlines, the time booked will be billed for in full.

LATE FEES/PENALTIES: All invoices are due **no later than 30 days** from the date of invoice. If an invoice remains outstanding more than 45 days past the date of the invoice then an additional invoice will be submitted with a $20.00 late fee; for each additional 15 days the invoice remains outstanding, an additional $20.00 late fee will be incurred.

INDEPENDENT CONTRACTOR CERTIFICATION: NorthWest American Sign Language Associates, Inc. is an S-Corporation and Tammera J. Richards, CI & CT; SC:L, NAD IV is an independent contractor and meets the following criteria for independent contractor status as defined by the IRS:
☑ ONLY works pursuant to written contracts.
☑ Works in more than three locations in a calendar year.

☑ Has a telephone and/or office listing that is separate from one's residence.

☑ Purchases advertising or business cards promoting one's business.

PAYMENT SCHEDULE: All payments will be made payable to: NorthWest American Sign Language Associates, Inc. EIN: XX-XXXXXXX

_____   _____
Tammera J. Richards, BS, CI & CT; SC:L; NAD IV   Service Requester

---

AGREEMENT TO CONTRACT FOR SERVICES:

I agree to contract for sign language interpretation and/or TypeWell transcription services with Tammera J. Richards, BS, CI & CT; SC:L, NAD IV under the outlined terms of service. I understand that this agreement constitutes the full agreement under which both the service provider and requester are bound. This agreement may be terminated by either party with written thirty (30) day notice to the other party informing the other of intent to sever the contract.

_____   Date_____
Tammera J. Richards, BS, CI & CT; SC:L, NAD IV

_____   Date_____
Service Requester

Tammera J. Richards dba NorthWest ASL Associates, Inc.
Street Address   Phone Number
City, State, Zip   E-mail Address

> **Tammy's Tip:** Avoid the use of the phrase "two-hour minimum," in your TOSA. To many people, this implies that you will be available and willing to work for a full two hours, when in reality, that is not what this phrase means to practitioners in our field. Instead, use the phrase, "initial fee" or "start-up fee" to avoid confusion. The point you are really trying to make is that you will not provide services for less than XX amount of money initially, and then, XX amount for each increment after that.

EIGHT

Billing Considerations

THE INFORMATION THAT IS contained in this section will help you avoid one of the most frustrating drawbacks of working as an independent contractor: delay in receipt of payment. These delays are often caused by neglecting to include information that the billing department needs or requires in order to process your payment. It is important to find out what is required, and make sure that information is included on the invoice to ensure timely payment.

Generally speaking, interpreters are classified by most service consumers (and payers) as "vendors." Often companies that receive other types of vended services such as purchase of stock and inventory, supplies, etc., have a set net term of 30 days. As previously mentioned, it is advisable to agree on the net terms of payment before provision of services occurs. It is also a good practice to ask up front for any forms that will need to accompany invoices (sometimes forms consist of independent contractor certification, travel/mileage reimbursement, or verification of service forms).

BILLING CODES

The following is a general list of possible forms or code numbers that could be required of interpreters at various sites:

- **AFPs** - Authorization for Payment vouchers. Often these are issued by state departments of Vocational Rehabilitation for services provided to individuals currently on VR caseloads. The required billing information that should be taken from the AFP and transferred to the interpreter's invoice is the AFP Number.

- **PCOs** - Purchase of Contract Order vouchers. Often these are issued by state departments of vocational rehabilitation for individuals seeking approval to be on VR caseloads. The required billing information that should be taken from the PCO and transferred to the interpreter's invoice is the PCO Number.

- **P.O. Number** - Purchase Order number. Usually service requesters will either inform the interpreter of the P.O. number verbally or via fax prior to or just after the interpreting assignment.

- **Case Number** - Case numbers are often used for state caseloads for Children's Services Division, or other advocacy type services. Sometimes caseworker signatures are also required for processing of payment.

- **Job Number** - Job numbers are often used by referral services that set up a job numbering system in order to track work performed in a given time period. Numbering systems vary, and requirements related to inclusion of job numbers on invoices are also at the discretion of the interpreter coordinator.

- **Social Security Number or Federal Tax I.D. Number** - one of these numbers is virtually guaranteed to be required. It is, in fact, so much a part of billing in most accounts payable departments (especially those which issue 1099 miscellaneous income forms annually to their independent contractors), that often interpreters have their social security or tax identification numbers printed on their invoice forms or statements.

- **Independent Contractor's Signature** - Some agencies require that interpreters sign their invoices. This is especially recommended for those individuals who run their invoices off an automated billing system on a computer. Businesses match invoices to pre-filled forms in order to prevent fraud, and also to verify the identity of the vendor. In previous editions of this book, I mentioned the option of submitting custom invoices that reflect your unique style. While this is still possible, I now feel that the paper you use, at least, should conform to the standard 8 ½ x 11" size. While you lose the uniqueness of non-standard paper, it is less likely your invoice will be lost or misplaced. Most computerized billing programs will allow you to paste a custom logo onto your invoice, so have no fear; there is still room for a bit of originality.

BILLING CYCLES

It is a crucial part of your business that you establish and maintain a billing cycle. This cycle is set at your discretion. Knowing when payment can be expected, you are able to gauge at what pace and how much income will be remitted. Thus you can determine your cash flow at any given time. If you rely on freelance interpretation for your primary source of income, setting up a schedule for billing is imperative in order to meet your obligations.

Some possible invoicing schedules include: billing after each assignment, billing on the 1st, 15th, or 30th of the month, when pay periods are established by referral agencies, or in any combination of methods as long as the method chosen is consistent, and recorded in your accounting program.

ADDITIONAL FORMS

Many entities, especially those run by federal, state, or local government, require supplemental verification forms in order to remit payment. Sometimes these forms are for the purpose of verification of the interpreter's presence, and other times the forms are for the service requester's information. When performing any assignment, be sure to ask the requester whether there are additional forms or documentation that are required, and if so, how they might be obtained.

NOTE: Any entity requiring additional forms should be willing to provide copies of necessary forms to the interpreter either by fax or by mail. If a master is provided for copying, the copying expenses are tax deductible as business expenses.

> **Tammy's Tip:** Tammy's Tip: Check your schedule on Sunday night for any appointments that may require forms, and fill out all forms that are needed for the week all at once. This saves time, and you will have them ready when you need them during the week. Also, keep a few spare forms in your car in case you accept a last minute assignment that might require one.

NINE

Tools of the Trade

THERE ARE A NUMBER of things you should consider when attempting to run your business efficiently. This chapter will cover issues such as useful technology for interpreters, logistical issues, office equipment, and organizational techniques.

TECHNOLOGY: MAKING OUR JOBS EASIER!

Historically, agencies wishing to contract for interpreting services had lists of interpreters they would call, one by one, to see if any of them were available for a given interpreting assignment. Since interpreters were out working during the day, they usually received their messages at night upon arriving home, and responded to calls as soon as they could. Currently, interpreter referral agencies use technology to their advantage by creating "all-page" lists and sending out job announcements to interpreters in bulk. Unless there is a specific request by the consumer, or a job requires specific skills for which not all interpreters are qualified, the general rule among coordinators is, "The first interpreter to call back about a job assignment receives the job." While there are pros and cons to this system, from a coordinator's perspective, it encourages a fast response on the part of the interpreters hoping for work. Another way technology has been used to improve communication between interpreters and agencies is by automating job confirmations, and allowing a visual form of job information to be sent to the interpreter quickly. Gone are the days of paper and pen, since information can now be sent nearly instantaneously to your wireless device.

Cell Phones/PDAs

With the advent of cellular phones and instant messaging technology, as well as e-mail and text messaging capability, the days of calling individual interpreters and waiting hours or even days for a response are long gone. If you want to operate effectively as a freelance sign language interpreter, it is an

ABSOLUTE REQUIREMENT that you have a cellular phone and/or personal digital assistant (PDA) device capable of sending and receiving text messages or e-mails of some length.

> **Tammy's Tip:** Check with your wireless carrier to find out whether or not they have an economical "unlimited data" plan. This will prevent you from incurring per-message charges when sending and receiving text messages, instant messages, or e-mails. Additionally, try to purchase a device that does not have a character limit on text messages that is so short you won't be able to receive complete pages from referral entities. Some devices have a 100-200-character text message limit, which is insufficient for receiving work information.

There are several reasons for carrying a cell phone or PDA. First, it is critical that you have the ability to call out to either the location to which you are providing services or the referral agency sending you to the assignment to inform them of late arrival, obtain directions, or prepare for assignments. Second, the bulk of an interpreter's work is paged out via text messaging, e-mail, or computer systems, and receipt of these pages is your means of receiving work. Next, many digital devices and phones have the ability to browse the Internet. This capability can allow interpreters to search maps, locate terms and vocabulary, or gain information about the entity to which they will provide services. Finally, when traveling a great deal, it is important to have the safety and security of a phone nearby.

> **Tammy's Tip:** When driving, DO NOT text message and do not talk on the phone without a hands-free set up. These practices are extremely dangerous and exponentially increase your risk of accident. Hands-free systems can be as simple as a wired or Bluetooth headset, or as complex as a Bluetooth system that is controllable through the console of your car via voice command.

When selecting a wireless service provider and accompanying wireless device, consider answering the following questions:

- What kind of coverage or service area does your wireless provider have?

- How easy (user-friendly) is the cellular phone or PDA you are considering buying? I recommend asking tech-savvy colleagues for their recommendations and finding out the pros and cons of various devices.

- What kind of reliability guarantees does your wireless service provider offer (do they have a good record for server up-time, or are there frequent data service outages)?

- What are the pros and cons of "all-in-one" devices such as Blackberries or Treos compared to having a stand-alone cell phone and some sort of PDA?

Tammy's Tip: Purchase a compatible car charger for your cellular phone or PDA. These chargers plug into your cigarette lighter, and allow you to rapidly charge your device for quick use. This prevents any unplanned lapse in communication due to a dead battery. Additionally, consider a wired or Bluetooth headset for hands-free use.

- What kinds of voice and data packages are available to meet your needs? Is nationwide, free roaming service available? What about unlimited data plans?

- What features are included with the phone or PDA (e.g., AIM, Yahoo Messenger, SMS (text messaging), camera, mp3, calendar, contacts, etc.)?

  Does the PDA or phone allow syncing to a computer for data backup?

Tammy's Tip: Think carefully about whether or not you want to purchase a phone or PDA that has a built-in camera. If you provide services in the court system, many courthouses and detention facilities will not allow you to bring in ANY type of device that is capable of transmitting pictures. Generally, the cameras on phones and PDAs are not high enough in quality to serve as your digital camera solution, so if this is an option you can live without, consider it.

GPS Systems

A second useful item for a freelancer to have is an in-car GPS navigation system. By no means is this a required item in order to be a successful interpreter; however, advances in this type of technology now offer various levels of navigation complexity to the interpreter constantly on the go.

Many new cars come with standard or optional in-dash navigation systems. While these are a great option, they are often quite costly. A more economical option is one of the many portable dash-mounted options made by Magellan, Garmin, or Tom Tom. There are literally hundreds of choices and configurations with a variety of features, including such options as a subscription to real-time traffic updates and re-routing, as well as mp3 players and photo viewers. Some of these GPS systems also act as hands-free Bluetooth speaker phone systems. While some systems are quite pricey, you can get an economical one that is portable (Read: You can use it in more than one vehicle and stow it when you aren't driving so it is not an attractive nuisance for thieves) for $200-$500.

> **Tammy's Tip:** Do some comparison shopping when considering the purchase of a GPS system. This technology changes rapidly, and there are many features that are non-essential and not worth the extra money. Look on sites such as Buy.com or Costco.com to find bargains. Check into whether or not services such as real-time traffic updating and re-routing require a subscription, and if so, what the cost is. Evaluate whether you really need features such as photo viewers and mp3 players combined with your GPS system.

Computers

A third critical piece of equipment for a successful businessperson is a personal computer. Whether you are a PC or Macintosh fan, you will find that having the ability to streamline your accounting and other office-related processes will require a home computing system. The form factor is all about personal preference. There are thousands of options in both desktop and laptop formats to suit your individual needs.

Tammy's Tip: Use your computer to back up the information on your PDA or cell phone into your Outlook or e-mail program. This way, if something unforeseen happens, like a phone falling into a toilet, your information and contacts will be backed up. There is no feeling like knowing you have to hand-input 500 e-mail addresses into your new phone or PDA.

You need only insure that your computer has the capacity to do the following:

1. Run a current computer operating system.
2. Run an accounting program.
3. Run a word processing program or suite.
4. Connect to the Internet via either wired or wireless connection.

Other peripheral pieces of equipment you will need include a printer, modem (preferably a high-speed cable or DSL connection), a monitor (if you are buying a desktop computer), and a CD and/or DVD burner (included in the desktop tower or laptop) for backing up data to CD or DVD periodically. Any other types of software or hardware you might want to purchase are at your discretion. You also will need to obtain Internet access through an ISP (Internet Service Provider). There are hundreds of ISPs to choose from, each with its pros and cons, and your options will vary by location. I highly recommend obtaining services from a high-speed (cable or DSL) provider if possible.

SCHEDULING SYSTEMS

Organization of interpreting appointments is one of the most key aspects of being a successful freelance interpreter. In order to maintain accuracy, attention to detail is paramount. While most scheduling is recorded electronically in PDAs, phones or other handheld devices, it is advisable to have some sort of backup or hard copy of your assignment and contact data in case of a catastrophic device failure. The following details some of the options available to you as a freelance practitioner.

Appointment Books

It is absolutely imperative that an interpreter carry a record of appointments scheduled. Interpreters often call their appointment books their "Bibles."

Appointment entries should include the following information[10]:

1. Time and duration of the appointment
2. Name of Deaf consumer(s)
3. Name and Phone number of the Contact Person
4. Address/Location of the Appointment
5. Job number or purchase order number (if applicable)
6. Billing address

Appointment books should be large enough to write a fair amount of information down, but compact enough to fit in a shoulder bag, purse, or briefcase. Keeping the book tidy is advised; it is annoying to all situation participants and embarrassing to the interpreter if bits of paper and scraps are falling out of the book.

Electronic Sync with Outlook or Calendar Program

Most PDAs and handheld devices will now allow you to sync your device with your desktop or laptop computer's e-mail or "calendar" program. This will enable you to maintain a data backup of the information you have on your handheld in case of data loss or interruption. It also allows you to print out a hard copy of your assignments on a daily, weekly, or monthly basis in order to have a written copy of your schedule. This can later be shredded once the assignments are completed to preserve confidentiality. My recommendation is to sync your device at least once per week and create a backup file of that sync no less than bi-monthly to avoid accidental data loss and huge headaches with data recovery.

Scheduling Follow-up Services

Sometimes, especially when interpreters are referred to assignments by an agency, it is required that an interpreter refer the service requester back to the agency with which the original assignment was coordinated, should further services be required. If the deaf consumer wishes to have the same interpreter for subsequent assignments, the interpreter should ask the service requester to contact the referring agency and request the specific interpreter. Never should an interpreter circumvent the referring agency and book with the service requester directly. Not only is this unethical, it will likely result in termination of your relationship with the agency.

---

[10] Be vigilant with your appointment book. It is important to minimize the amount of confidential detail stored within so as to avoid inadvertent disclosure of confidential information.

Interpreter Request Forms[11]

When taking down the information for an interpreting assignment, it is extremely helpful to utilize some type of request form. This form should list all the questions that an interpreter would normally ask in order to be prepared for a potential assignment. After this form is filled out, all information is completely listed, and there is little chance of forgetting to ask an important question.

These types of forms can be customized to match the needs of the individual interpreter. Included on the sample Interpreter Request form in the Appendix are the types of questions that should be asked.

LOGISTICAL CONSIDERATIONS

"Oh no! It's a PowerPoint presentation!" Probably one of the most dreaded events for any interpreter is working in a situation where total darkness could happen. It is vital that information about this type of presentation be given to the interpreter in advance. In the event that a slide show, Power Point, video presentation, film, or overhead projector is going to be used, there are a number of ways to make the event accessible to all consumers in a given situation.

Similarly, in performance art events, or platform interpreting situations, there are ways for interpreters to have the best auditory access to information without causing any major upheavals. For more information on interpreting in theatrical or performing arts settings, reference the book, *Sign the Speech,* by Julie Gebron, CI & CT; NAD IV.

Here are some strategies for working in challenging situations like those described above[12]:
- **Bank Lighting:** If a presentation is taking place (especially a slide show, Power Point, video, or overhead), lights can be shut off in various areas of the room in order to make the area near the interpreter visible.

---

[11] See sample request form in "Sample Forms."
[12] Any and all of these suggestions can be made to the service requester. It is not an expectation that the interpreter would do all the legwork, but that he/she would be perceptive enough to ask questions and incite the requester to action.

- **Spotlighting or Specials:** The size of an event and its location will dictate whether or not theatrical lighting can be used. Often a spotlight (with a gel over it to minimize glare), set large enough to frame the interpreter from the top of the head to mid-thigh and at full arm-span, will allow enough light. **This is not a suggested lighting technique for interpreters working in a theatrical performance.** Another possibility is to have a "special," or a light that is especially rigged for the interpreter in a specific area and is usually controlled separately from other lighting. This solution is a good one when a light board is being used in an auditorium or large hall.

- **Video Presentations:** If at all possible (for example, in a classroom setting or workshop setting), scan materials and syllabus schedules for indication of video presentations. If they were taped from public access or are recent videos produced by the Department of Education there is a possibility that they have been captioned. **It is worth it to research this!** Make sure a caption decoder or captioned TV can be located, or find out if the videotape or DVD is offered in an open-captioned format.

- **Ambient Lighting:** Often, an interpreter can make use of what is known as ambient lighting. This can be light spill from a nearby window, or the use of a portable light such as a clip-on book light or mini-mag light that can be aimed at the interpreter and provide additional light to the Deaf consumer. Sometimes, depending on the setting in which an interpreter is providing services, a music stand with attached light can be used to provide ambient lighting to the interpreter.

- **Auditory Access for the Interpreter:** There is nothing worse than standing on stage or in a cavernous gym and having to sign, "I'm sorry, I can't hear/understand what they are saying." The echo and depth of a room will have a great effect on what kind of interpretation is possible. To offset this possibility, ask that a monitor be placed on the stage **facing the interpreters** so direct input can be accessed. Make sure that there is no chance of feedback from other equipment.

If the event is a large concert, wireless monitors are even better. They resemble headsets but are more compact. A clip-on receiver is worn on the belt or put in a pocket.

There is better technology being developed in this area all the time. Remember to speak with the sound engineer or have your contact person do so to resolve the issue of auditory access. Furthermore, **insist** on a **test** of the system.

- **Visual Access for the Interpreter:** One of the most challenging things for interpreters is accessing visual information that is being presented behind them. The time it takes an interpreter to turn around and look at the visual information can cause delays in message rendition and can cause confusion on the part of both the interpreter and the Deaf consumer. One piece of technology that has become available for interpreters to address this issue is called the Interpreter Mirror, and is marketed by ClearView Innovations http://www. clearviewinnovations.com/. This device reflects the source material to the interpreter, allowing the interpreter to avoid having to turn around to view it.

Tammy's Tip: If you are interpreting for a large event, arrive at least 30 minutes prior to the event in order to speak with the sound and lighting technicians about lighting the interpreter and making sure that the event is audible (placement of a monitor facing the interpreter or use of a wireless monitor). It is advisable to arrange these types of logistical items with the service requester well before the event since lighting and sound designs are often completed well ahead of time. When speaking with sound and lighting technicians, be clear about what you need, and try to work in as collegial a manner as possible.

TEN

Video Relay Services and Video Remote Interpreting

VIDEO RELAY SERVICES (VRS)

ACCORDING TO THE Federal Communications Commission (FCC) website[13], video relay services are defined as the following: a form of Telecommunications Relay Service (TRS) that enables persons who are Deaf or hard-of-hearing, and who use American Sign Language (ASL), to communicate with voice telephone users through video equipment rather than through typed text. Video equipment links the VRS user with a TRS operator – called a "communications assistant" (CA) – so that the VRS user and the CA can see and communicate with each other in signed conversation. Within video relay services, the CAs are referred to as video interpreters or VIs. Because the conversation between the VRS user and the CA flows much more quickly than with a text-based TRS call, VRS has become an enormously popular form of TRS.

Here is how VRS works. The VRS caller, using a television or a computer with a video camera device and a broadband (high speed) Internet connection, contacts a VRS CA, who is a qualified sign language interpreter. They communicate with each other in sign language through a video link. The VRS CA then places a telephone call to the party the VRS user wishes to call. The VRS CA relays the conversation back and forth between the parties — in sign language with the VRS user, and by voice with the called party. No typing or text is involved. A voice telephone user can also initiate a VRS call by calling a VRS center, usually through a toll-free number.

The VRS CA can be reached through the VRS provider's Internet site, or through video equipment attached to a television. Currently, more than ten providers offer VRS. Like all TRS calls, VRS is free to the caller. VRS providers

---

[13] http://www.fcc.gov/cgb/consumerfacts/vrs.html.

are compensated for their costs from the Interstate TRS Fund, which the Federal Communications Commission (FCC) oversees.

The benefits of VRS are as follows:

- VRS allows those persons whose primary language is ASL to communicate in ASL, instead of having to type what they want to say.

- Because consumers using VRS communicate in sign language, they are able to more fully express themselves through facial expressions and body language, which cannot be expressed in text.

- A VRS call flows back and forth just like a telephone conversation between two hearing persons. For example, the parties can interrupt each other, which they cannot do with a TRS call using a TTY (where the parties have to take turns communicating with the CA).

- Because the conversation flows more naturally back and forth between the parties, the conversation can take place much more quickly than with text-based TRS. As a result, the same conversation is much shorter through VRS.

- VRS calls may be made between ASL users and hearing persons speaking either English or Spanish.

There are some important points to remember about VRS. VRS is different from some of the other forms of TRS in two important ways: (1) the conversation between the VRS user and the CA is made through a video link and sign language, rather than typed text; and (2) the service relies on the Internet, rather than the telephone system, for the connection between the VRS user and the CA. It is a relatively new service and, unlike some other forms of TRS, state provision of VRS services is not mandated by federal law as of publication of this book. Here are some things you should know:

- Preferential treatment of calls is prohibited. VRS (and TRS) providers must handle calls in the order in which they are received. They cannot selectively answer calls from certain consumers or certain locations.

- Unlike with some of the other forms of TRS, the VRS CA may not be able to offer or handle some call services, such as operator-assisted calls and 900 (pay-per-call) calls.

- For emergency calls (for example, calling the fire or police department), a VRS CA may not be able to automatically direct the call to the appropriate emergency service provider or know the caller's location. TRS and VRS should not be used for emergency calls. Emergency calls should be placed by dialing 911 directly on a TTY using the regular telephone network.

- The TRS rules do not require the user to choose or use only one VRS provider. The user can choose any of several different providers of VRS.

- Accepting VRS equipment from one provider does not prohibit the user from using another VRS provider on other equipment the user may have.

- A VRS provider may not install VRS equipment so that the user's Internet connection works only with that provider's equipment, unless the user expressly agree to this.

- VRS (and TRS) providers may not offer the user financial incentives to use their service or to make more or longer VRS (or TRS) calls.

- VRS is not the same as Video Remote Interpreting (VRI). VRI is the use of an interpreter located at a remote location through a video connection when two people are together and they need an interpreter. VRS may not be used in such circumstances. VRS is a type of telephone call.

Speed-of-Answer and 24/7 Requirements for VRS

The FCC has adopted various rules to improve VRS service. Speed-of-answer requirements were phased in during 2006 and took full effect on January 1, 2007. Now VRS providers must answer 80 percent of all VRS calls within 120 seconds. VRS providers must also offer the service 24 hours a day, seven days a week.

For more information on VRS and TRS, consult the Disability Rights Office of the Federal Communications Commission (FCC) and learn more about FCC programs to promote access to telecommunications services for people with disabilities. The Web site is www.fcc.gov/cgb/dro

VIDEO REMOTE INTERPRETING (VRI)

Video remote interpreting (VRI) is similar to VRS interpreting in that it uses video conferencing technology over the Internet to provide interpretation services to Deaf and hearing consumers. However, it differs in several important ways.

➲ Video remote interpreting services are **not** regulated or funded by the FCC.

➲ Providers of video remote interpreting services generally use a fee-for-service model or charge on a per-minute basis since they are not reimbursed via surcharges collected by the Interstate TRS fund.

➲ When using VRI services, the sign language interpreter is stationed at a remote location, but the Deaf and hearing consumers are usually located in the same room. During a VRS call, Deaf and hearing callers MUST be in different locations in order to receive services.

➲ VRI services are **not** mandated by the federal government, and are **not** regulated in any way (as of the publishing of this book).

Many people have asked me about the viability of VRI for personal remote service provision from one's home. While it certainly sounds like an appealing option, there are several things to consider before deciding whether or not establishing a VRI service is right for you as an individual practitioner. Currently, there are several interpreter referral agencies around the country that are offering VRI on a larger scale, with the VRI equipment being housed in their offices rather than in individual interpreters' homes. I do believe that this option will become more and more viable as technology advances.

Some of the issues to consider when evaluating VRI as a service provision option include:

➲ High-speed Internet Connection: Do you have a reliable (99.999% reliability) Internet Service Provider (ISP) who has a guaranteed level of service? Can that ISP supply you with sufficient bandwidth at a reasonable price? Will the ISP provide you with a static Internet Protocol (IP) address in order to prevent connection difficulties?

⮎ Do you have the appropriate quality of equipment? Usually, your standard webcam does not provide a fast enough frame rate to allow VRI to work. You need a minimum of 30 fps (frames per second) in order for signing to be viewed smoothly, without pixelation or drag. Less than this, and there are bound to be comprehension problems on both sides.

⮎ Do you have the technical expertise to deal with troubleshooting firewalls and dealing with port settings, or do you have the ability to develop a web-based application to circumvent such issues?

⮎ Are you computer and audio-visual savvy?

⮎ How do you troubleshoot issues such as not being able to hear the hearing participants or see the Deaf consumer? How do you deal with having multiple consumers?

In addition to these questions, there are ethical questions that must be considered such as:

⮎ In what types of settings is VRI appropriate?

⮎ In what types of settings is VRI **not** appropriate?

⮎ At what age can VRI work in educational settings?

⮎ Is there a possibility that service requesters will begin to rely on VRI for all services and stop using in-person services when in-person services best serve the consumer(s)?

⮎ How do you handle coordination of a team interpreter, if needed?

IMPACT OF VRS AND VRI ON THE FIELD OF INTERPRETING

While VRS and VRI are remarkable new technologies that have opened up many new opportunities for Deaf consumers and interpreters alike, the advent of these services and the numerous full-time interpreting jobs that go with them has drastically impacted community interpreting.

With the great influx of VRS companies, the number of interpreters working as community or freelance interpreters has diminished greatly. This means that rather than driving from job to job, and running one's own business as an independent contractor, interpreters are now opting for taking part- or full-time employee positions with VRS companies that are offering insurance benefits and paid time off. As more centers open across the country and in Canada, the dearth of interpreters in the community and in K-12 school settings is felt even more acutely. So while Deaf people have full access to VRS services to make doctor appointments, they now face difficulty in finding interpreters to appear **at** those appointments. This is a situation that will not soon be resolved.

The field of interpreting continues to face a critical shortage. Demand continues to **far** outweigh the supply. More VRS companies continue to establish themselves, and interpreters continue to be drawn away from the uncertainty of freelancing to the guaranteed hours and salaries of VRS work. So how do we serve both needs knowing that interpreters are a finite resource, and knowing that we want the security of VRS work plus the variety and community commitment of freelance work?

My solution is to provide some of both. I work part-time at a VRS center, while also providing freelance interpreting and TypeWell Transcription services. This gives me the variety and community interaction of freelance interpreting, while still allowing me a guaranteed base of hours at the VRS center. This solution isn't for everyone, however, and you need to decide what the best fit is for you. Remember, flexibility and diversity in your skill set makes you a more valuable service provider.

Finally, a word about qualifications for VRS. In my opinion, it is critical that you have at least 3-5 years experience as a sign language interpreter (preferably certified) before applying to work in a VRS center. The exception to this might be if you were able to enroll in a mentorship program offered by the VRS center at which you were interested in working. VRS requires highly developed closure skills, the ability to understand a wide variety of Deaf consumers from across the United States and Canada (and sometimes, beyond!), along with being able to operate and technically troubleshoot computer technology. Getting some experience in three-dimensional (face-to-face) interpreting will ultimately help prepare you for the challenges of two-dimensional interpreting (VRS/VRI).

ELEVEN

Vicarious Trauma and the Interpreter:
One Valuable Perspective

WHEN DETERMINING WHAT additional topics I wanted to include in the third edition of this book, I decided that one issue that is largely overlooked is vicarious trauma to the interpreter. Vicarious trauma is defined by McCann & Pearlman (1990) as,

> A stress reaction experienced by therapists and researchers who are exposed to disclosures of traumatic images and materials by clients and research participants, in which therapists or researchers experience enduring changes in the manner in which they view self, others and the world. Additional terms often used to describe vicarious trauma: secondary traumatic stress, secondary traumatic stress disorder, compassion stress and compassion fatigue.

Like therapists and researchers, interpreters are privy to traumatic disclosures by virtue of their involvement in highly charged, emotional interpreting settings, as well as through their repeated exposure to the oppression of a minority group; that is, Deaf and hard-of-hearing people, by majority culture members; that is, hearing people.

While I have experienced vicarious trauma as an interpreter, I am not a psychologist and don't feel that I am the most qualified person to introduce this topic. Therefore, I have enlisted the help of Dr. Michael Harvey of Framingham, Massachusetts to enlighten the readers of this text about this critical issue affecting practitioners in our field. Dr. Harvey is the Co-Director of a private, non-profit organization, **Dialogue Toward Change**, located in Framingham, MA. This organization is dedicated to providing research, training and consultation services to alleviate the potentially negative impact of witnessing oppression. He earned his Ph.D. in Clinical Psychology from the University of South Dakota in 1978, and has been a psychologist in private practice specializing in deafness and hearing loss since 1980. Dr. Harvey can be contacted directly via his website at: http://www.Michaelharvey-phd.com.

Two articles follow, both written by Dr. Harvey: "The Hazards of Empathy: Vicarious Trauma of Interpreters for the Deaf[14]" and "Shielding Yourself from the Perils of Empathy[15]." I find these articles insightful and validating for interpreters.

As an interpreter, please remember that your mental health is important. If you find yourself experiencing symptoms of depression or other types of psychological distress, don't hesitate to enlist the help of a qualified therapist, doctor, or mental health professional. It is impossible to be effective in our jobs as facilitators if we are plagued with personal issues that could bleed into our work. Getting the right help will allow you to continue your interpreting career without dreading what the next day might bring.

---

[14] This is an expanded version of an article appearing in the *Journal of Interpretation* (2001), 85-98. Feedback is welcomed by Dr. Harvey at 14 Vernon St., Suite 304; Framingham, MA 01701; mharvey2000@comcast.net. For website survey, go to http://www.Michaelharvey-phd.com.

[15] This is an expanded version of an article appearing in the Journal of Deaf Studies and Deaf Education (Spring, 2003), 8(2), 207-213. Feedback is welcomed by Dr. Harvey at 14 Vernon St., Suite 304; Framingham, MA 01701; mharvey2000@comcast.net.

The Hazards of Empathy:
Vicarious Trauma of Interpreters for the Deaf

Michael A. Harvey, Ph.D.

"They were ignoring the Deaf consumer!" Donna exclaimed.

"And what was that like for you?" I asked.

"Well, at first I thought that there was something wrong with my interpreting and I felt guilty and inadequate. But the deaf person told me that my signing was really clear." In spite of over ten years experience as a certified interpreter, Donna's first inclination was self-doubt.

"Please tell me what happened, as if it's happening in the present tense."

"Well, the meeting started -"

"The meeting is starting," I reminded her.

"Uh, sorry. The meeting *is* starting in the conference room. There are about 10 hearing people sitting around a long table along with Dick, who's deaf. I'm sitting across from him so he would be more included in the meeting. It starts off okay; people are talking one at a time; he's following everything and he even makes a few comments. But then someone cracks a joke and everyone starts to laugh. Since I'm still interpreting what they were saying a few sentences before, I miss the joke. I ask them to repeat it, but the team leader says something like 'John's just being a wise ass, let's go ahead.' Dick doesn't seem to mind but I feel bad for him.

"Then the pace of the meeting increases, people use English idioms and they begin talking out of turn. I notice I'm sweating. But Dick's sitting there patiently and looks lost."

"What thoughts do you have about Dick's patience?"

"Well, I don't know if I consciously thought of it right then, but maybe it pissed me off a little bit. He should speak up, too, and get all of them to talk in turn. Otherwise, he's stuck out in right field. I'm also thinking that I should say something."

"They put him out in right field and you're angry at him and yourself for letting them do that."

"Yeah. And I'm also royally pissed off at the hearing coworkers for not caring. No one gives a shit!" she yelled. By this time, Donna's face lost its composure and became flushed. With a tight clamped thrust, she slammed her fist down on her knee.

An amazing but not surprising phenomenon: how an *ordinary* act of oppression—one that we observe on a daily basis—can cause such an *extraordinary* reaction for those who bear witness to it. (If I had a nickel for every instance that we hearing people talk out of turn and make accurate interpretation impossible for deaf people, I would be a rich man). It is more self-evident how observing the effects of newsworthy trauma—i.e., disasters, abuse, murder, etc.—would cause marked distress. But while the effects of observing mundane oppression and defamation are more insidious, they are no less profound. This is the focus of the present paper. Interpreters for the Deaf routinely interpret in situations where a Deaf consumer is subtly or overtly oppressed, humiliated or otherwise demeaned.

There is a cost to caring, particularly for those who have the capacity for compassion and empathy. Donna found herself overwrought by an internal combustion of thoughts, feelings, and behaviors, which included self-condemnation, rage and self-injurious behavior.

"So what do you do with a deaf person's pain?" came my deceptively simple question.

"Come again?" Donna replied.

"It seems to me that consistent and close-range observation of oppression must cause certain psychological and behavioral responses in anyone.

You *cannot not* do something with pain. The vicarious trauma of Deaf peoples' pain *must somehow affect you.* To quote Carl Jung, 'trauma is contagious.'"

"Well, I know that when I feel badly for someone, I want to help; I want to make their pain go away."

"And?" came my gentle prompt.

"And sometimes I can't."

"Your bubble is burst. No matter how hard you try, you're confronted with your inability to ultimately take away the pain of another or to change the conditions which cause it."

And "I often find myself feeling inadequate," she added, "because I can't change the world. And it's particularly during these times that I have trouble saying 'No.'"

The Victim, Oppressor, and Bystander Hazards

The interpreter as a victim. Donna had begun to discuss an extremely common hazard of interpreting: the self-victimization stance. This refers to the largely unconscious tendency to sacrifice one's health as an attempt to compensate Deaf consumers for times when other hearing persons have oppressed them. To take care of oneself is to feel selfish: "What right do I have to take care of myself when Deaf people undergo...?; How can I enjoy life when others are suffering?" Accordingly, interpreters may work under unhealthy conditions, when they are seriously ill and at jobs that trigger intense trauma and hurt. They put themselves at high risk for a variety of debilitating psychological and physical repercussions.

Many interpreters report varying degrees of depression as well as other debilitating psychological symptoms. Post-trauma reactions are particularly common. It is a well-known phenomenon among therapists, for example, that the mere knowledge of another's trauma can be traumatizing! Indeed, Psychologist Charles Figley defined vicarious trauma as "the natural consequent behaviors and emotions resulting from knowing about a traumatizing event experienced by a significant other; it is the stress resulting from helping or wanting to help a traumatized or suffering person." (Figley, 1995).

For example, all too frequently an interpreter routinely interprets under unhealthy conditions—way beyond half-hour stints—in spite of consistent warnings from the medical community. Carpal Tunnel Syndrome, as well as other forms of repetitive strain injury, is a direct result of such compulsive work behavior. In my work with interpreters, I have come to understand the dynamics of these physical conditions as psychologically driven; as a form of self-victimization largely resulting from witnessing oppression without adequate emotional support. In essence, *repetitive strain injury is a symptom of untreated vicarious trauma.*

Researchers have coined the term "physiological synchrony" in reference to the fact that our minds (emotions) and bodies (physical reactions) are intimately intertwined and interdependent. Empathy has a definite physical component; in fact, one psychological researcher defines empathy as "an autonomic nervous system state which tends to stimulate that of another person." Our nervous systems, in other words, "talk" to each other. When a mother plays with her infant, their hearts begin to beat in time. When you pet your dog, your heartbeat slows down – and so does your dog's. And when you empathize with a deaf consumer who is oppressed, your nervous system becomes tense (Ciaramicoli & Ketcham, 2000).

Burnout is another common and related manifestation of self-victimization, also often oversimplified as "stress-related." However, typically burnout is a gradual process of emotional exhaustion, whereas vicarious trauma can emerge suddenly and without warning. But the effects are similar. When we help others without also helping ourselves, we become physically, psychologically and spiritually impaired. I am reminded of the consistent announcement from stewards on airline flights: "If the cabin pressure changes and an oxygen mask appears, make sure you give yourself oxygen before your children." Depleted helpers are incapable of helping anyone.

There is an ambiguous line between compassion/altruism and co-dependent behavior. Many interpreters may unwittingly come to rely on helping others *at their own expense* in order to gain self-respect, particularly to assuage their self-loathing for having failed to expiate oppression, past or present. *Co-dependent behavior* is a common coping strategy that we use when our self-esteem is threatened. It feels good to gain the respect of a community, to be valued and even needed. One's own sense of self-competence and skills are enhanced. But what comes is only a short-term "high" unless we do the necessary psychological work on ourselves, in essence the psychological version of giving ourselves oxygen.

The interpreter as an oppressor. In addition to victimizing ourselves, what else might we do with pain that we cannot hold? Answer: we may project it on to others so they can hold it for us. Being accused of oppression typically causes guilt and shame for those of us who pride ourselves on our enlightened and liberated attitudes. Nevertheless, it is something we all do, to a greater or lesser degree, to assuage our pain. We often "unfairly," albeit unconsciously, project onto our friends and lovers what we cannot handle or "hold" ourselves.

If an interpreter is unable to tolerate his/her own discomfort and sense of inadequacy—perhaps about one's inability to eliminate oppression or ordinary evil—that individual may project those feelings onto other interpreters by deeming *them* incompetent. I'm okay; you're *not* okay. Note the frequent observation of backbiting in the interpreting community; i.e., "S/he signs ASL poorly, is lazy, ill-intentioned or has an attitude." Much like many groups who are under stress or oppressed themselves, there is marked competition and tension among members of the interpreting community, largely because of the heretofore-uncharted effects of vicarious trauma.

Other interpreters are not the only possible targets of one's projections. Deaf consumers also are natural targets. Here one "gives" one's inadequacy to a deaf consumer(s) to "hold" by deeming that person(s) as cognitively, emotionally and/or behaviorally defective. One interpreter, for example, complained that a deaf consumer was "much too concrete to stand up for his rights"; or that she "had a chip on her shoulder." Consequently, the interpreter made decisions for the deaf consumer by insisting on what level and kind of interpretation she needed, even when that consumer protested.

An important aside: An interpreter's negative assessment of *specific* colleagues and *specific* deaf persons may be accurate—i.e., an interpreter may be incompetent and a deaf person may be immature—and this assessment may, in some cases, be one's ethical obligation to point out. However, the gusto, fervor and intensity of the criticism often falls markedly short of being supportive and ethical in nature; it is properly termed as oppressive behavior, possibly even vindictive. But to emphasize again, that behavior does not necessarily reflect the interpreter's incompetence or meanness; it is a common consequence of observing the defamation of others. Specifically, oppressive behavior partially stems from a normal, unconscious human proclivity to project those negative traits on to others what we cannot tolerate in ourselves.[16]

Human service providers are particularly vulnerable to this dynamic. A common built-in risk to helping is that we may unwittingly get angry at those who do not appreciate our good efforts. It is frequent observation, for example, that those clients who have been traumatized by previous caregivers or significant others are likely to be critical of subsequent help. Rather than risk repeated emotional abandonment, they will lash out and reject the helper before s/he has a chance to do the rejecting. The best defense is a good offense.

To the extent that a deaf person has been mistreated and/or traumatized by previous hearing helpers, that person's reactions to a hearing interpreter will fall somewhere on the continuum from mild caution to blatant mistrust to active hostility. This sets the stage for a complicated and uneasy cross-cultural exchange. If an interpreter primarily depends on a deaf consumer for validation of his/her competence, a deaf person expressing anger or frustration—whether it be reality-based and/or of displaced origin—often sets the stage for intense anxiety and anger.

Hurt and outrage are commonplace. In particular, an interpreter may complain that Deaf people are ungrateful; i.e., "they don't recognize the hard work that we do." Indeed, it is hard work to learn American Sign Language, about the Deaf community, Deaf culture, and so on. As a neophyte interpreter put it, "In my ITP, I worked my ass off with hopes and dreams for a long and fulfilling career. But now deaf people make me feel like I shouldn't even be in the profession! Although I know that they bash hearing people because they've been oppressed so much, I certainly didn't do anything wrong. They can go

---

[16] Blaming the victim is an old story and, unfortunately, a universal human phenomenon. Harlan Lane reviewed the scientific literature on the "psychology of the deaf" from the last few decades, comprising some 350 journal articles and books, and found it rife with negative stereotypes, such as "immature," "concrete," "egocentric," "rigid," "passive," "intellectually inferior" and "emotionally immature." Analogous to what we do as individuals, our society projects pejorative characteristics onto certain groups—in this case, deaf people—rather than "tolerate" relevant noxious and oppressive conditions.

shove it! They're so immature!" Note that this interpreter ended her outcry of hurt by becoming oppressive through imparting a negative stereotype. But to emphasize again, it's not that the interpreter was a bad or an oppressive person per se. Oppressive behavior is one natural consequence to feeling overwhelming pain.

The Interpreter as a bystander. Rather than react to pain by self-victimization or oppression of others, another common vicarious trauma response is to erect a shell of protective numbness. It can be argued that one reason Sigmund Freud positioned his chair in back of the couch was to avert eye contact and emotional involvement with his patients with the rationalization it helped them to free associate. Perhaps Freud was unconsciously overwhelmed by the emotional material that would inevitably come up during psychoanalysis. Similarly, in the early days of the interpreting profession, a "machine model" was in vogue with a similar rationalization of avoiding unnecessary interpreter interference in the situation. Although there is much validity to that view, it also provided a safety barrier; the interpreter could avoid feeling helpless and struggling with how/when/if to take action in the face of oppression and even stark abuse of the Deaf person.

Although professional distance and objectivity are certainly necessary, there is the omnipresent danger of becoming too callous and indifferent to the Deaf consumer. In the trauma literature, we hear of "affective constriction" or "affective numbing"; our psyche unconsciously goes on "tilt" in the face of overwhelming trauma. A more descriptive term is "compassion fatigue," an internal separation of thought from feeling which depletes one of any sympathy/empathy for others: "We have a job to do, a salary to earn; and what's the fuss about advocacy, commitment and compassion anyway?"

Instead of integrating the vicarious trauma, such defenses are aimed at "disposing" it into one's unconscious—in effect, to make believe the event had never happened. The delete and trash barrel computer icons come to mind. Although the "What I don't think about can't hurt me" attitude gives us the comforting illusion of not being "brought down" by another's pain, our shield —our running away from our own vulnerability—in fact insidiously leads us to a *self-imposed exile*. Unlike with computers, the traumatic memory—the "file"—never quite gets disposed of or deleted. Instead, we constantly have to hold down the lid as our discomfort threatens to erupt into consciousness.

The squelched traumatic memory becomes a continual energy drain, a leach. Failure to acknowledge and to work towards integrating a trauma, while giving us some protection, it is temporary and ultimately saps us of life.

•••

Back to Donna. "So we have listed some effects of vicarious trauma, but not yet some of the reasons. Why do you become so tormented?" came my admittedly direct query.

"I usually don't," Donna countered.

"So why is this situation different from all other situations?"

"Because we eat only unleavened bread?" she jested in a mock Yiddish accent. We exchanged a knowing smile, each of us recalling the similarly-framed four questions from the Jewish Passover Seder. I flashed back to my uncle who every year—immediately after asking "Why is this night different from all other nights?"—would pontificate how "We recall the horrors of slavery and relive our suffering as a way to inspire future transformation." I had no idea what he meant. But as a child, my entrepreneurial ambition was to invent a way to inspire transformation (whatever that was) without having to suffer. I would be rich and famous.

"Seriously, though. What about being an interpreter contributes to your torment?"

A long pause. This time she gave my question some serious thought.

Empathic injury

"Well," Donna began, "interpreting, by necessity, means to focus on the needs of the deaf person. My job is to break down the language barrier that isolates him or her."

"You'll have to tell me if this is true since I'm not an interpreter. But I've been told that accurate interpretation partially depends on your ability to achieve a certain empathy, or so-called 'empathic attunement,' with a Deaf consumer; to have a strong sense of how he or she feels during the exchange that you're interpreting."

"Yeah," she nodded her head. "For some reason, I'm not as affected by this stuff when I'm interpreting for a group of deaf persons. Witnessing oppression gets under my skin more when I'm interpreting for an individual. Weird, huh?"

"It isn't weird," I replied. "We humans are hard-wired to empathize more with an individual person than with a more abstract group of people. And as you said, your empathy with a given person is essential for proper interpreting. There are emotional hazards to empathy, however; you can be traumatized as a result of caring."

The hazards of empathy have been covered in my other chapter entitled "Shielding Yourself from the Perils of Empathy" and will not be repeated here.

"Let's put the hazards of empathy aside and get some other occupational, emotional hazards of interpreting on the table. We can explore each of them in more detail later. Tell me, how has it been for you to witness ordinary evil?"

Grieving the Prevalence of Ordinary Evil

"What do you mean by 'ordinary evil'?"

"Everyday kinds of evil—rudeness, disrespect, lying, exploitation, etc.— that aren't severe enough to make CNN. But nevertheless, they leave an impact on you."

"I'm a bit confused by your term *ordinary* to describe evil. To me, evil is anything *but* ordinary. But I do see what you listed all the time. Like deceit, people cutting in line, road rage, sexism, someone deliberately sabotaging your success. Even kids pulling legs off of bugs or frogs just for fun!" She then added a final observation: "And frankly, although I know I should be used to it by now, every once in a while, it still comes as a shock; that evil is so close, so pernicious!"

In fact, ordinary evil happens frequently in our presence and forms the backdrop of our daily existence. Often it is barely noticeable. Indeed, the evil in our time is the loss of consciousness of evil.

Sometimes, however, that evil suddenly rears its ugly face; it comes as a rude shock and offends us. Like Donna, many people experience that "rude shock" as a kind of developmental crisis of coming to terms with the ordinary evil that they witness *close up.* In contrast, evil done far away "not in my backyard" is easier to ignore. Interpreters for Deaf persons do not have that luxury. Although, on an intellectual level, we all know that the world isn't fair, nevertheless face-to-face unfairness often comes as a visceral betrayal.

"It really bothers me to see a deaf person oppressed," Donna observed while tightening her wrist.

"What about deaf people being oppressed touches you the most?"

"It's wrong! It's mean! It's not right! It's evil!" Again her face became flushed and her hand formed a fist.

"Is that one reason you became an interpreter?

"Of course! In addition, I was intrigued with ASL, the culture..." She listed several other more academic reasons. "And yeah, I also wanted to lessen oppression, to make the world a better place."

No Innocent Bystanders

"And given that you not only witnessed oppression but were also part of it, what do you say to yourself about yourself?"

"Well, I know I couldn't stop it," she slowly responded. "I mean, I could have said at that meeting 'Hey, one at a time' which I do many times. But ultimately, I couldn't force those people to repeat themselves."

"So rationally, you had no reason to doubt yourself or to feel like you were letting Dick down."

"If my life were only rational," she sighed. "I can still see the blank expression on his face when people began talking over one another."

"What do you think he was feeling?" I asked.

"Probably big-time helplessness. Like no matter what he or I could do, nothing would change. The hearing world doesn't give a shit about deaf people!"

"So he's angry, too?"

"Yeah, I'm damn sure he's angry!" Donna shouted. "But he's used to experiencing what you call ordinary evil. He probably has adapted to it, numbed out to it. Ironically, I probably feel worse about it than he does!"

Donna thought for a minute and looked toward the wall. "And I do very much wonder about what part I played in this scenario?"

"What do you mean?" I asked.

"When I told Dick's co-workers that I couldn't interpret their too-fast and out-of-turn chatter, all they said was that it wasn't important or 'Never mind.' And I kept on interpreting while they denigrated and ignored him more. After a while, I felt like I became one of them!"

"First you felt exploited by the hearing power base to maintain their status quo and then kind of felt like you became one of them?"

"Exactly!" Donna proclaimed with an emphatic nod. "There are no innocent bystanders. Even though there wasn't anything I could have done to make them respect Dick, I somehow felt like a perpetrator."

"Say more," came my invitation.

"They were guilty. They could have and should have slowed down. They weren't going too fast inadvertently; they knew damn well what they were doing! And I didn't stop it. That makes me feel as guilty as them."

"Guilt by association?"

"That's part of it," Donna winced. Then she looked down toward the floor.

Reconciling One's Privileged Majority Status

"And sometimes," she continued, "I even feel guilty leaving the situation—joining my family, going to a nice house, nice friends, and comfortable life. Like I should be doing more."

"No matter how much you do, there's always more?" I asked.

"Yeah, particularly because I'm very fortunate. I have a good life. I feel guilty for enjoying life when I see how much the deaf consumer struggles."

"It's complicated," I responded. "What you're describing is a sort of guilt-by-association that comes with belonging to an oppressor group. It seems to me that part of wrestling with the vicarious trauma of interpreting is how you reconcile belonging to a privileged majority; how you justify going home to your four bedroom, two car garage home with the knowledge that the oppression will happen again and again."

Donna shook her head sadly. "That's the bitter truth. I enjoy my life. The last time that I personally experienced oppression was when the 1:00 matinee was sold out; I had to wait for three hours!" Her sarcasm was evident.

"And that wasn't even directed at you!" I smiled. Donna's words seemed straight out of Albert Memmi's book, *The Colonizer and the Colonized* (Memmi, 1965), in which he reminded us that members of an oppressor group, like it or not, are viewed as having higher status, are afforded greater privileges, and indeed consciously or unconsciously exploit their position. Our economic position shapes our lives. As Malcolm Forbes put it, "Money isn't everything as long as you have enough."

Fearing the Big Mistake

"And not only do I feel guilty about not doing enough," Donna continued, "but what if I make it worse?"

"What's the 'it'?" I asked.

"A deaf person's oppression. In addition to sometimes feeling guilty about abandoning deaf people, I can't get the fear of 'What if I make an interpreting error' out of my mind and..."

"Excuse me," I interrupted. "What do you mean 'if'? You mean somehow you will work for however many years and won't make any errors?"

"No, of course not. But I'm afraid I'll make the *big mistake*! And then the Deaf person will suffer more than ever! The RID lightning bolt will strike me dead."

"Russian roulette?"

Donna nodded her head emphatically and again tensed her arms and wrists. The beginning stages of Carpal Tunnel, I thought. I thought of a vascular surgeon who emphasized to his residents that "you have to connect each and every vessel together perfectly; there is absolutely no room for even a minute error!" While that doctor's unerring, hyper-meticulous approach is certainly appropriate for surgery, it causes debilitating anxiety for human service professionals—i.e., interpreters—whose craft is both scientific/exact and creative.

"What if you could believe that doing the best you can is good enough? Would your wrists and arms be less tense or more tense?"

"It would be a relief," Donna affirmed. "But it's hard for me to do."

"I know it too well, " I sighed.

A true story: During a vicarious trauma and interpreter conference, Ann felt overwhelmed and decided to take a drive. However, as "luck" would have it, she was one of two cars out of over 100 that were blocked in. So she walked around the lake instead; and, in a short time, decided to sit on a rock. Soon she noticed a butterfly right above the water line trying without success to fly. It was obviously injured.

"I found a stick and lifted the butterfly up," she recounted. "It flew for a second, only to fall down a little further in the lake. I then found a longer stick and again lifted it up. Again it flew for an instant and fell into the water. With a still longer stick, I helped it again but it was in vain. And soon the butterfly was out of my reach."

"Then I knew that I did all I could do. I had to let it go."

Family-of-Origin "Unfinished Business"

"So let's switch gears a bit," I motioned to Donna. "When you witnessed Dick's co-workers ignoring him, where did it bring you back to?"

"That's easy," Donna quickly replied. "I remember many other times that hearing people ignored deaf people by ."

"I mean you personally. What experiences have you had being ignored?"

"Well, we're all ignored sometimes," she rebutted, perhaps with a hint of defensiveness.

"That's certainly true," came my deliberately short response. I invited her to continue.

"Are you talking about my childhood?" she asked.

"If that's where you go when you see deaf people being ignored," I replied.

"Well, my father was an alcoholic. I wished he would have ignored me *more* because he was very abusive when he got drunk. I certainly didn't feel ignored by him. I was the oldest and it seemed that he picked on me the most. I had to deflect his anger from going on my younger brother. My mother needed me..."

"And what did your mother do before, during and after he got drunk?"

"She waited on him hand and foot; she did anything to keep him from drinking!"

"And when she was waiting on him hand and foot, what was she doing for you?"

"Nothing. She was too busy taking care of him. I was too busy taking care of my brother and mother." Donna's eyes gazed upward as she accessed old memories. Then she made eye contact and grimaced.

"And what was that like for you?" I continued.

"It felt lonely for sure. And ironically, in some ways that felt worse than my father's abuse."

"I believe it was Martin Luther King who said, 'In the End, we will remember not the words of our enemies, but the silence of our friends.'" She nodded her head repeatedly and came close to tears. She had made the connection, both in her head and now in her heart. Donna had identified with Dick and had reacted to the hearing co-workers as she had toward her own mother. Transference happens to everyone, including therapists, interpreters and probably even vascular surgeons.

Many helping professionals have been parentified in some way as children, frequently feeling obliged to assist their parents in ways beyond their means. I have learned from my research on Vicarious Trauma and Interpreters that many interpreters often unwittingly continue old family patterns of sacrificing their needs, but now in their vocational lives. In Donna's case, as well as for others, she relived old, painful family scenes of her emotionally neglectful mother during the routine of doing her job.

It was time to return to the subject of Dick. After again making eye contact with Donna, I asked, "What did you imagine Dick was feeling while he was being ignored at the meeting?"

"I dunno, maybe confused. I'm sure he had no idea of what was being talked about. I was interpreting everything the best I could, but it wasn't enough. I remember him nodding his head with a blank look on his face."

"And what do you think he was feeling?"

"Helpless, stuck, stupid, overwhelmed, despairing, worthless, isolated, disconnected..." Donna had no shortage of words. She then affirmed what we both had already discovered: "I know those feelings well."

"Your profession is challenging, both in the technical aspects of interpreting and in the emotions it evokes." Donna nodded her head.

"It all sounds so negative," Donna interjected. "Aren't there any positive effects of witnessing oppression?"

"It doesn't have to be all negative," I replied. "Like many things, if vicarious trauma is managed correctly, it becomes an asset, a blessing."

Donna shook her head and wistfully said, "I wanna invent a way to avoid the suffering and get right to the blessing part."

"Me, too," I admitted, remembering my uncle's sermons at Passover— "We recall the horrors of slavery and relive our suffering as a way to inspire future transformation"—and my childhood entrepreneurial wish to inspire that transformation without having to first suffer. "But that's not the way it works," I lamented with Donna. We exchanged a knowing glance.

Endarkenment

"It's probably a good thing," I continued. "If you learn how to manage vicarious trauma correctly, it indeed can benefit you in many profound ways. It becomes a *transformative experience*. On the other hand, if you don't manage it right, it can kill you."

"An obvious choice," she smiled.

"But one that many people don't realize they have." I told Donna about a Jungian analyst, Jean Shinoda Bolen, who once led a group of women into an underground cavern. They were told to sit still for hours without light or discussion. Upon returning to the "light," nobody reported enjoying the experience of darkness; everyone experienced degrees of terror. But they all reported benefiting tremendously from the ordeal. The group coined the term "endarkenment" to describe the archetypal wisdom that comes with going into the darkness and coming back again.

"Well, I heard there're some caves nearby in New Hampshire. We can call the Chamber of Commerce," Donna joked.

"Too much of a tourist trap," I volleyed back. "But your vicarious trauma is a potential cave. As you witness oppression, your world abruptly becomes darker and more ominous. But your cave is potentially transformative. It can enrich you, particularly as you realize that the world, in fact, hasn't changed at all. Instead, you have relinquished a naïve but developmentally necessary innocence about the invariable goodness of humanity."

The changer and the changed. There is a Buddhist saying that when the student is ready, the teacher will come. If an interpreter" is "ready," bearing witness to a Deaf consumer's oppression contains many invaluable opportunities for "endarkenment." The lessons are several. Having access to a richer, dualistic and more complex view of the world, we have an opportunity to learn about our own duality as well; to explore that which makes us feel proud and that which causes us shame. As one interpreter put it, "I've come to realize that my bearing witness to respect and disrespect, joy and sorrow, laughter and pain is at the heart of what it means to be human."

There is Goethe's Faustus story, written almost 200 years ago in 1808. Faustus, who was revered by everyone in his kingdom, was celebrating his good fortune with all of his subjects. It was a perfect day with perfect music, libation, ornate decor and so on. But at the height of all the pomp and circumstance, a smelly, wet, dirty dog ran in and promptly jumped on the King, threatening to ruin the event.

However, the King did not attempt to rid himself of this burden, but *embraced it!* He realized that he needed to come to terms with—to *integrate*—his dark, disowned side, symbolized by the dog, before he could attain true wisdom and happiness. Faust needed to examine and integrate his pain in order to feel whole and fulfilled. It is an *essential duality.*

Our capacity to be fully human ultimately depends on understanding and integrating duality whether we witness it in ourselves, in interpreting situations or in our daily lives. In addition, our vicarious trauma can expand our boundaries of self to encompass the outward world. It serves as a catalyst for us to struggle with how and why oppression exists; to question whether one is complicit in perpetuating it; and to grapple with ways of minimizing it. An interpreter's ethical mandates are challenged; i.e., "What I am able, willing and obliged to change about the world; how I can counteract the oppression of Deaf persons in ways that do not contradict the intent of the RID Code of Ethics."

Integrating vicarious trauma can provide meaning to one's life, a raison d'etre. To quote Hillel's famous passage, "If I'm not for myself, who will be for me? If I'm only for myself, what am I? If not now, when?" For example, Eli Wiesel incurred the vicarious trauma of witnessing his father being murdered by Nazis. Partially, as a result, he has dedicated the rest of his life to help ensure that no other Jews can similarly be murdered. Interpreters, too, practice what is called Tikkun Olum, a Hebrew phrase which means "to fix or repair the world." Via an ally model, interpreters advocate for Deaf persons for whom and with whom they're working.

Through the understanding of oppression—and our potential responses to it—we experience a freedom which is redeeming and which holds us responsible to live in dignity amidst those whose actions are undignified. We learn that it is the small gestures we make, often subtle, perhaps gentle but direct and honest, that will weaken the actions of those who would unfairly and wrongly treat another. Perhaps it is this benefit that keeps many interpreters in the field.

> Donna looked puzzled. "So exactly *how* do you manage your vicarious trauma so it becomes transformative experience without it killing you?"

> "The first step—one that's the most important and perhaps the most difficult—is to recognize it. Don't pretend that you aren't traumatized."

> "Is that all? Just know that I've been traumatized?"

> "Know it; don't deny it. Understand the complexities of it. And talk about it a *lot* with supportive others; give it words."

References

Ciaramicoli, A. P., & Ketcham, K. (2000). *The power of empathy: A practical guide to creating intimacy, self-understanding and love.* New York: Dutton.

Figley, C.R. (1995). Compassion fatigue: toward a new understanding of the cost of caring. In B. H. Stamm (1995). *Secondary traumatic stress.* Lutherville, MD: Siddran Press.

Memmi, A. (1965). *The colonizer and the colonized.* Boston, MA: Beacon Press.

Shielding Yourself from the Perils of Empathy

Michael A. Harvey, Ph.D.

I WILL NEVER FORGET when my 5-year-old daughter was first stung by a bee. I swear it hurt me more than her. This experience of vicarious pain is not felt by parents only, but haunts anyone who feels compassion for another human being in anguish. In the words of Czech author Milan Kundera,

> There is nothing heavier than compassion. Not even one's own pain weighs so heavy as a pain with someone and for someone, a pain intensified by the imagination and prolonged by a hundred echoes.

Interpreters are typically highly compassionate people who are besieged by a hundred echoes of Deaf peoples' pain. As one interpreter put it, "We have a built-in over-sensitivity to oppression of Deaf persons that's installed into our psyches before or during our interpreter training." While the components of this "installation" are quite intricate and often elusive, I will artificially demarcate some of them for clarification. These conclusions are largely based on interpreter training workshops that I have conducted and a website interpreter survey (http://www.Michaelharvey-phd.com) which, at this writing, has yielded over 80 responses.[17]

A glimpse into another's soul. Compassion invites empathy: the desire to imagine the inner workings of another person's psyche; to "put your ear to another person's soul and listen intently to its urgent whisperings. *Who are you? What do you feel? What do you think? What means the most to you?*" (Ciaramicoli & Ketcham, 2000). When we feel the pain, in Kundera's words,

---

[17] As this is ongoing research, readers are very much invited to reply. For this website survey, please go to http://www.Michaelharvey-phd.com.

"with someone and for someone," the ripples of their pain permeate our psyche, just as the ripples of a stone permeate a body of water.

With empathy we not only deeply connect with another human being, but also are simultaneously, ever so subtly, changed ourselves. Empathy necessarily catalyzes self-transformation. In my case, I imagined that my daughter thought the bee sting would kill her; "Daddy, daddy! What's happening to me? This hurts! I don't wanna die! Daddy, why won't you help me? Help! Help!" Perhaps she didn't think and feel any of these things—it happened so quickly. Perhaps I was oversensitive. But I'll never forget how *I* felt as a witness, even though Emily got stung over ten years ago. (She doesn't even have any memory of the event!). My empathic pain permanently changed me somehow, ever so subtly.

"That's all very interesting," one interpreter politely interjects, "but we're supposed to be neutral. Otherwise, we wouldn't be doing our jobs."

"Do you have a character disorder?" I ask.

"Excuse me!" she responds, this time markedly less politely.

"I didn't mean any disrespect," I'm quick to clarify. "In fact, it was a clumsily phrased compliment. People who have so-called 'character or personality disorders' may not have the capacity for compassion. But most of us are psychologically healthy and therefore inevitably feel another's pain and joy. For most of us, thank God, it's impossible to be neutral."

"But I'm an interpreter, not a counselor," the interpreter persists.

"Right. So there's a paradox here: you're supposed to be neutral but this is impossible. When in the close presence of someone in pain, you cannot not have some degree of empathy; it is an involuntary psychological reflex. There's a tension of boundaries: machine versus ally model. But that's your department, not mine. From a psychological perspective, however, I think the issue is more how you *manage your non-neutrality:* what you do with the inevitable fact that you care."

As interpreters – at least from a psychological perspective – you not only inevitably have to care, but I've been told that you purposely empathize with a deaf consumer(s) as a routine part of your job. In one interpreter's words, "Competent interpreting necessarily depends on your ability to sense how a deaf consumer feels during a particular linguistic exchange." Accordingly, it is no surprise that when I ask interpreters to *think back to a situation in which a hearing person somehow oppressed a deaf consumer,*" they—like my recalling Emily getting stung—have no difficulty coming up with a slew of oppressive situations that have stayed with them even after several years have elapsed. A few examples:

- A Deaf consumer is left out of a conversation or decision-making.
- A Deaf consumer is talked down to and demeaned.
- A Deaf consumer is treated unfairly/unjustly.
- A hearing consumer is uncomfortable with an interpreter and ignores him/her to the detriment of the deaf person.
- A hearing parent makes fun of a deaf child's signing.
- A Deaf consumer being falsely labeled as mentally retarded.
- A Deaf consumer being physically and/or emotionally abused in a treatment or correctional facility.
- Being asked to unethically expand my interpreting role to the detriment of the deaf consumer.
- Discrimination by hearing officials; misuse of power.

"It's difficult to pinpoint how observing oppression has affected me, but it has," one interpreter began. "I can only begin to imagine Deaf people's helplessness and squelched rage against the onslaught of hearing dehumanization, devaluation, and degradation. It leaves me with chronic indigestion."

That interpreter's metaphor of "chronic indigestion" is quite fitting, as the psychological literature on trauma often refers to un-integrated affect as *"undigested material"*; and as a result, subsequent material (life experiences) cannot get properly digested (integrated). In other words, following the witnessing of oppression, one may then be oversensitive and overreact to subsequent similar experiences. A constant state of red alert.

An important caveat: oppression versus ignorance. It is important not to overstate or exaggerate the prevalence of oppression done by hearing people to deaf people. Not every instance of apparent malfeasance is driven by oppression, which by definition implies intent. Ignorance and naiveté are also common culprits. Indeed, as I have stated elsewhere (Harvey, 2001), to the extent that an apparent incident(s) of oppression is traumatic to an observer, that observer may be hypervigilant for its reoccurrence – s/he may perceive oppression when it, in fact, is not there. Indeed, this is one hallmark symptom of vicarious trauma (Pearlman & Saakvitne, 1995), a common "cost of caring." From a psychological perspective, *anyone who frequently bears witness to oppression is at higher risk for becoming hypervigilant to its occurrence.*

Although there are many instances of hearing people—arguably the majority! —who, because of their naiveté or inexperience around Deaf persons, *unintentionally* act in detrimental or unhelpful ways, (intentional) oppression of various forms and degrees is prominent in the lives of Deaf people (Harvey, 2003; Glickman & Gulati, 2003; Pollard, 1998; Lane, Hoffmeister & Bahan, 1996; Lane, 1984). Accordingly, bona fide instances of oppression will at least be familiar to interpreters and others who bear witness to the experiences of Deaf persons.

Contrasting extremes of affect. Your "over-sensitivity" may also be intensified by its juxtaposition to the Deaf person's apparent *under*-sensitivity, much like a bright, iridescent color stands out against a gray background. This theme is echoed in the following dialogue between an interpreter and a Deaf colleague:

Interpreter:	"I can't believe that you weren't promoted at your job. You couldn't get more training because they didn't have an interpreter!"
Deaf colleague:	"Surprise, surprise" (with resigned sarcasm).
Interpreter:	"It's infuriating!" (with aggressive outrage).
Deaf colleague:	"I'm used to it."
Interpreter:	"Well, I'm not!"

The interpreter's heightened pain was triggered by his anger upon observing the Deaf colleague's apparent numbed resignation. That deaf person's reaction of "being used to it"—also known as affective constriction or numbing out

—is a common adaptation to prolonged stress or trauma; e.g., to cultural insensitivity, discrimination, disrespect, disregard, etc. Unfortunately, for many deaf people, these adversities have become a staple of their lives. Continually blinded by the "bright, iridescent colors" of oppression, their world is reduced to shades of gray.

Not so for hearing people, which includes most interpreters. At least when we first enter the field, we are not "used to it." We are appalled and outraged about our "audist" society's subtle and not so subtle denigration of deaf people. In my own case as a psychologist, I was shocked to learn about many deaf persons' experiences of communicative isolation within their hearing families of origin; these images haunted me, angered me and pained me. They intruded into my leisure "off work time" and into my dreams. Many years later, I understood these symptoms as indicative of Post Traumatic Stress Disorder: the cost of my caring (Figley, 1995). I discovered that trauma is contagious.

Projective identification. You may also feel intensified pain because—in a psychological sense—the deaf person gives it to you to "hold." I am reminded of a cartoon depicting a couple on an airplane. One spouse asks the other, "Do you want to be scared on this trip or should I?" The cognitive-emotional sequence may go as follows: First, the husband feels overwhelming fear that the plane will crash. Too proud to internally or publicly acknowledge his feeling, he projects it on to his wife: "She is afraid, not me!" In this manner, he can identify with the fear that he imagines resides "in" his wife. He then may unconsciously encourage or reinforce such fear responses in his wife; e.g., by making anxious body movements. And, in turn, the wife finds herself feeling increasingly uncomfortable. In a psychological sense, she "holds" her husband's disavowed fear.

This psychological phenomenon, called "projective identification," happens quite frequently between any two people who are emotionally connected to each other. Stated most technically by Melanie Klein, projective identification occurs when a subject displaces a part of the self—e.g., one's unacknowledged, unwanted feelings—onto another person and then identifies with that person or encourages a response in the person that corresponds to the original feeling.

What part of *the self* might a deaf consumer displace onto an interpreter? Consider the case of Mattie, a middle-aged deaf woman who had a long history of rejection and painful ordeals: her parents were emotionally unavailable, her husband had multiple affairs and divorced her, and most of her previous employment settings had failed to provide even minimal work accommodations. On the surface, however, she looked remarkably unscathed: she seemed very confident, remained socially active, was ambitious and enjoyed high self esteem. She did not surrender to her pain-engendering hardships.

So was it a coincidence that many competent interpreters found themselves feeling grossly inadequate while interpreting for Mattie? As one interpreter observed, "I don't know why, but I just feel awful about myself when I'm with her. It's nothing she really says or does, or at least I can't pinpoint it. But I feel her critical eye on me, and it's like she makes me feel inept!"

Although Mattie's resiliency was impressive, it is difficult to imagine that she was pain-free. And given that she felt a level of pain, the question becomes what did she do with it? (Pain doesn't just evaporate). I don't think it was coincidental that many highly competent interpreters felt "grossly inadequate" in Mattie's presence. Like the wife on the airplane, it seemed that an interpreter(s) became a "container" of sorts for Mattie's unwanted or disavowed affect. Via projective identification, Mattie displaced those pained, incompetent parts of her self onto the interpreter and then acted in certain ways to encourage that response in the interpreter.

Projective identification happens without malice; Mattie did not consciously wish for the interpreter to feel her own pain, nor did the interpreter consciously agree to accept it. Shared pain occurs unconsciously for both parties, without informed consent. In this manner, an interpreter is likely to get "sucked in" before s/he knows what's happening. And its effects are profound, particularly as the pain is "intensified by one's imagination."

Again to return to my memory of my daughter getting stung, part of what I'll never forget is her eyes fixated on me as she writhed in pain. In retrospect, I sensed Emily pleading, "Please, please share it with me! I can't endure this alone!" I'm quite sure she didn't know about projective identification back then; but she probably did it anyway. Somehow we humans seem "hard wired" to share pain in this way. *Shared* pain is always better, at least for the one who is the original holder of it.

The dual nature of empathy. By now you should imagine big red warning signs saying, "Empathy prohibited. No trespassing." Indeed we can ask "Aren't we better off protecting ourselves on our own well-defined turf?" "Who needs the weight of compassion or empathy, particularly if we end up 'holding' some of it for another person?"

The story of Medusa from Greek mythology offers guidance. Medusa was a beautiful maiden who attracted many suitors. In one version of this myth, she was raped by Poseidon, ruler god of the sea. And from then on, because of Medusa's burning rage pouring from her eyes, those who looked directly at her would turn to stone. Proper precautions needed to be taken, such viewing a reflection of her off a shield. Interestingly, Medusa was also worshipped as a great serpent goddess who had intense wisdom and an ability to see through one's illusions to the truths that rest behind. In this tradition, her face was hidden since to look upon it was to see one's death, as Medusa saw into your future.

Although my referencing this myth may seem like a non sequitur to the reader, its relevance to understanding the hazards and benefits of empathy should soon become clear. A preview: Unless you are aware of the vicarious trauma risks and take proper precautions, empathy with someone in anguish can metaphorically turn you to stone. However, with the proper tools—metaphorically, a shield—one can gain intense wisdom and access to profound truths. Perhaps the most basic tool/shield is to balance the *emotional* and *cognitive* components of empathy. How you balance the dual nature of empathy will largely determine whether you reap benefits (gain wisdom) or incur danger (turn to stone). This is illustrated in Figure 1.

Figure 1. **Empathic balance.**

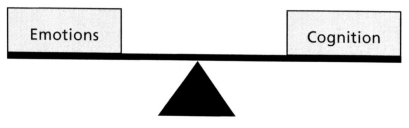

First, let me clarify the *emotional* component of empathy. Pure, unbridled emotional empathy, without any cognitive constraints, is akin to achieving a state of psychological fusion with another: the mystical experience of two separate bodies/minds melding together as one. Many people achieve a transitory, heightened state of fusion during sexual passion when two bodies become one; others during intimate conversation: i.e., "He thinks my thoughts, completes my sentences." Others resort to drug use; for example, with hallucinogens, which cause the boundaries of self and other to temporarily collapse. Although elusive and abstract, pure emotional empathy is perhaps the most sought-after of all human experiences.

There is more good news. By empathizing with another person, without restraint, we overturn author Thomas Wolfe's verdict that "Loneliness... is the central and inevitable fact of human existence." On the contrary, we experience that "people need people"; that empathy is good for your health. In more technical terms, Object Relations Theory emphasizes that empathy satisfies two kinds of essential psychological needs; 1) *merger needs:* feeling totally at one with another with a complete loss of boundaries and separateness; and 2) *alter-ego needs:* a need to feel an essential alikeness with another significant person.

We have noted that, as interpreters, you practice empathy as a necessary part of your job (Harvey, 2001). Actors also have such opportunities and provide an important comparison. Perhaps the most concise description of how professional actors empathize with their characters was elucidated by drama coach Lee Strasberg. He developed a specific procedure, called "Method Acting," to teach actors this very skill. Method actor Shelley Winters advises prospective actors to empathize with a character by "acting with your scars." In other words, when an actor portrays the multi-dimensions of a character—including those deepest, most frightening or painful experiences written by the author—the actor has to find similar experiences and relevant memories in his or her own life, be *willing,* and then be *able* to relive those experiences and memories onstage as the "character."[18]

Method acting may be called a "How to Empathize" manual, whether it be for actors, interpreters, or anyone else for that matter. An important

---

[18] From website, http://www.theatrgroup.com/methodM/

124

query: If competent interpreting, like acting, demands this kind of affective empathy and if empathy indeed is "good for your health," why don't actors, interpreters, etc., reap only the potential benefits of empathy? Why isn't the necessity to empathize with the deaf consumer all good news: a "win-win"! Doesn't the deaf consumer benefit by accurate interpretation while the interpreter benefits by a growth experience?

It's not that simple. If you experience empathy solely via your emotional faculties, then you're in danger of affectively drowning, of becoming deluged, flooded and overwhelmed with too many emotions; you lose yourself. Or per the Medusa myth, it turns you into stone. Total fusion without boundaries is *bad* for your health. Consider the experience of one high school interpreter:

> I was interpreting a meeting between a deaf student and his hearing teacher. The teacher treated the student in a very patronizing way, very disrespectful. I remember thinking what a total asshole he was. But I had to convey to the student exactly how he was being an asshole: his body language, his facial expression, his tone of voice, etc. Although I know it's my job to give the affect of the speakers, I felt torn portraying this awful teacher's words. I felt dirty being a part of the communication.

Again, in the analogous case of method actors using relevant memories to empathize with their characters, it is significant that Strasberg himself recommended that the actor use memories that are at least seven years old in order *to avoid risking psychological trauma. Interpreters do not have that luxury.* Although it is certainly possible, and often important, to temporarily put aside traumatic memories during an interpreting job, it seems difficult at best to screen out what memories get activated. Whereas actors have many hours of prep time before going on stage, you interpret affectively-laden material in "real-time, spontaneous improvisation." To quote one interpreter, "I have enough to worry about—transliteration; voicing what he's signing; using the right words, inflections and body language; signing in his style what's being said; being an ally, etc., etc.—without even noticing, never mind worrying about, what personal memories get triggered!"

This is where the cognitive component of empathy becomes important. Whereas the emotional component of empathy has to do with merger and symbiosis—"I feel your feelings, think your thoughts"—the cognitive component has to do with disengagement, with holding onto your integral sense of self as *distinct from another.* The cognitive component is your metaphorical shield that keeps you safe.

Specifically, while experiencing the emotional fusion of empathy, it is vital to *cognitively* remind yourself who you are. One interpreter noted, "Sometimes when I'm really affected by a deaf consumer's pain, I rub my forehead just to remind myself that I'm still here." Allowing herself to *emotionally* feel his pain had to be balanced by her *cognitively* holding on to her sense of self. "Even though I feel like him, I know I'm *not* him."

It was not coincidental that the above interpreter used touch to ground herself. There is an old saying that one way to know you're alive is to stick yourself with a pin; or the popular expression that "I pinched myself to make sure I wasn't dreaming." Similarly, the psychological literature on dissociative disorders describes many tactile techniques of "waking a person up" from a trance or dissociative state, essentially in order to "remind yourself who you really are." When my then 5-year-old daughter had night terrors – a common childhood dissociative state – I would touch her forehead so she would wake up and "remember" who she really is.

In another context, there is a story told by Primo Levi about his imprisonment by the Nazis. When he was close to despair and considering giving in to death, he took care to wash his face every day. It was the one volitional act that he, and *he alone,* could control. And thus, it helped restore his identity, apart from the oppressive context. It reminded him who he was; that he was still alive (Groopman, 1997).

There are many ways to cognitively remind yourself who you are in addition to using physical touch. These are variations of enacting what we can control over our body, mind and soul. At interpreter workshops, I do an adaptation of the following guided meditation:

> Imagine that you're interpreting for a deaf person who's being oppressed in some way: shafted, cheated, demeaned, and ignored.

There are many possibilities. You become overwrought and consumed with that person's pain. You're in danger of being devoured by it, drowning in it. You feel your own self becoming smaller and smaller and threatened with total annihilation.

As a trusted safety measure, you recite to yourself what you're able to control.

I can control the rate of my breathing.

I can control where I touch my body.

I can control how and when I wiggle my toes (My fingers are too busy interpreting).

Focusing on what I can control is one way of reminding myself that I'm me; I'm not the deaf person; I am myself!

I may like chocolate or vanilla, maybe neither. Regardless, I am me.

I have a favorite color. I am me.

I can control what I learn about myself from this job. About the world. About humanity.

Regardless of how much pain I see, I can be *curious*.

These are the parts of me—and many more—that I bring to the interpreting situation.

Balancing the dual nature of empathy—the "I feel your feelings" with "I am still me"—is often easy-to-say but hard-to-do, particularly in times of stress and when psychologically traumatic memories get activated. In my view, it is this challenge that is metaphorically illustrated by the Medusa myth. It is not surprising that nobody could look directly at Medusa without turning to stone; that instead, one could look only at her reflection off, for example, a shiny shield. Imagine the pain and rage that "poured from Medusa's eyes" following her rape by Poseidon! Imagine the pain that she "gave someone to hold"!

One of the profound lessons that the Medusa myth offers is that there are inherent dangers of emotionally empathizing with another's pain without holding on to our "shield" of self-affirmation. In other words, we must ensure that another's pain reflects *off of our psyche;* that we understand and empathize with another's pain as it resonates within ourselves; as it brings up *our own* issues, *our own* life experiences, *our own* thoughts and feelings. "I can differentiate your pain from my own." It is via this delicate emotional and cognitive balance that we can safely put our ears to another person's soul and reap many profound empathic benefits.

What happens when one's empathic pain is "intensified by the imagination and prolonged by a hundred echoes" without being balanced by helpful "self-talk"—the "shield" of cognition? Figure 2, The management of empathy, illustrates one possibility.

Figure 2. **The management of empathy.**

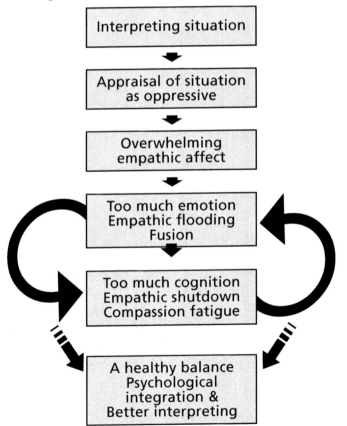

An example of too much emotion: I recall a conversation with an interpreter who struggled to regain empathic balance as she felt deluged by emotions while witnessing a deaf patient getting inadequate care in a psychiatric hospital. In the interpreter's words, "Those asshole hearing doctors diagnosing Mary as paranoid was horrible!" In this case, the interpreter had appraised the reasons for oppression as driven by evil and malice as opposed to well-intentioned naiveté.

"And what was that like for you?" I asked.

"I couldn't stand it! She was so helpless! She had absolutely no power; she was raped by the system, put in a cage, imprisoned, labeled... Mary also probably felt..."

"I asked you about your feelings, not Mary's. Please say more about you not being able to 'stand it,'" I interjected.

"Watching her being misdiagnosed and labeled was horrible," came her persistent but poignant reply.

"Can you step back for a minute and analyze where your feelings come from? What experiences of yours does Mary's predicament activate?"

After a moment of thought, the interpreter discussed in some detail her own childhood ordeals of being falsely labeled with Attention Deficit Disorder (A.D.D.) when, in reality, her boredom and inattention were due to incompetent teachers.

"So your sense of Mary's pain of being misdiagnosed is reflective of your own similar experience?"

"Yeah, I know the feelings all too well," she replied.

"Let's examine the similarities and differences between your experience and Mary's; then you can really 'step in her shoes' and interpret as many of her linguistic and emotional nuances as possible, but not melt into her in the process. It sounds like up to now you've been overwhelmed with her pain."

She nodded her head and sighed.

This interpreter had been in danger of empathically drowning, one possible negative consequence of unbridled empathy, which we have discussed. Typically in this scenario, we become depleted of energy; we withdraw from family, friends and colleagues, perhaps accentuated by the belief that no one could possibly understand our distress; and, in the case of interpreters, one may also withdraw because of misinterpreting the RID code of ethics as prohibiting the discussion of any thoughts and feelings concerning an anonymous Deaf consumer(s). We experience profound alterations of our identity, self-esteem, and worldview; our ability to manage strong feelings suffers; and we are vulnerable to intrusive imagery and other post-traumatic stress symptomatology. In short, we are vicariously traumatized.

An example of too much cognition.

Another common vicarious trauma response is erecting a shell of protective numbness. It is a safety barrier, a way of hiding, a way of shutting one's eyes to the blinding empathic pain of witnessing oppression. We become overwrought with compassion fatigue: a self-protective shell of isolation behind which we look out for only number one, caring for nobody else but ourselves (Figley, 1995). It is a common response among helpers who regularly deal with people's pain without adequate self-care. As one seasoned oncologist put it, "I never thought I'd dehumanize my patients as disease entities, but after witnessing so many deaths, I'm tired of caring!" An experienced acute care nurse observed, "The faces of the patients at the ER become all one big blur." And as one seasoned, highly compassionate interpreter put it, "When I first learned about oppression and deaf people, I was appalled and outraged. But after a while – and I'm ashamed to say this – I sort of got used to it. You ask me about empathy! What's that? *I have no empathy!"*

There is no need for shame. Rather, "getting used to it" is a human response; overwhelmed with grief, we become tired of caring so much. Gradually and insidiously, the stories of Deaf persons' isolation and denigration may become a routinized expectation, the norm. What begins as a contrasting extreme— and therefore catalyzes reactions of astonishment, shock, distress, concern and torment—gradually succumbs to the weight of passive resignation. After a while, we come to expect such oppression. And in my case, more often than I, too, can easily admit, I hardly notice its existence.

In marked defiance of Milan Kundera's statement that "There is nothing heavier than compassion," we hide our faces in the sand. We reduce piercing, iridescent vicarious pain to a gray, dull ache; but, in the process, we become non-feeling machines. Thoughts replace feelings. We tell ourselves, however, that it's a small price to pay, as we revel in never having to ever again agonize over another's sorrow.

One interpreter admitted that "I got to the point that when I saw something too horrible or painful, rather than have compassion or struggle with my emotions, I would go over my shopping list! – Not just as a coping technique, but, to be honest with you, it actually felt much more important to me than the deaf person's pain or even worrying about the adequacy of my own interpreting."

"Your shopping list is a hell of a lot simpler than empathy."

"A lot simpler and a lot less painful," she agreed.

Typically, our cognitive retreat into our own versions of "shopping lists" does not last long. For one reason or the other – most of the time we don't know exactly what hit us—the intensity of another's pain permeates our self-made fortress, and we again acutely feel the omnipresent malignancy of oppression. The good news is that we again feel alive; and the bad news is that we may not have the tools to find a healthy balance between empathic flooding and empathic drought. That is the challenge.

On achieving a healthy balance. On the one hand, I have come to be distrustful of simple solutions and prescriptions: "if only you will do so and so...". On the other hand – at least as far as I've been able to figure out – many profound solutions, when boiled down to their essence, are simple-sounding; that is, although their implementation is anything *but* simple, they first present themselves as such. With this caveat, I will conclude with some concrete recommendations.

Here is one simple-sounding prescription: talk about your feelings with supportive others; don't keep them bottled up. One of my favorite principles of healing is: *"Pain has a size and shape, a beginning and an end. It takes over only when not allowed its voice."*(Brener, Riemer & Cutter, 1993) The more words we have for our empathic pain, the more shape it has, the more it has a beginning and end. The less words, the less space; the more it takes over; the more we're vicariously traumatized.

In my opinion, it is a common but serious error to assume that one can get helpful support only from those who already understand, who are in "the same [interpreting] boat." First, as many interpreters have noted, there are many ethical ways of sharing one's emotional reactions with non-interpreters without violating the RID Code of Ethics. Secondly, as anyone who has been in a long-term committed relationship knows, it is often the *struggle* to help another dissimilar person to empathize with you that is the healing medicine; that catalyzes you to verbalize and clarify all the nuances and complexities of a particular stressful situation. People from Mars also need people from Venus. We need both supportive others who are similar – i.e., peers, consultants, supervisors—*and those who are dissimilar* – i.e., friends and spouses.

Many interpreters have reported benefiting greatly by journal writing – another form of dialog, at least with symbolic-others. For me, writing has become a necessary and healing labor of love that helps me put into words some of the most important things I have come to believe as well as what I'm in the process of trying to figure out. But equally important, or perhaps more so, is that I have long realized my need for another to react to me, whether positively or negatively—whatever! In some ways it doesn't matter, for that dialog is an essential part of my balance.

In addition to this simple-sounding advice, let me suggest an attitude shift that I have found helpful in my own work while witnessing oppression. When I find myself overwhelmed with "isn't this awful, this shouldn't be," and potentially debilitating anger/pain—while continuing to empathize with the victim and asking myself what I can do-- I adopt an attitude of a *curious anthropologist*. This attitude of curiosity is my "shield"; that which I use to protect myself from unguarded exposure to the "eyes of Medusa." I nurture a desire to deepen my understanding of what it means to be human, including the parts of me that I learn about. Emotionally rough encounters then become data, grist for the mill. There's an old sailing expression: "The difference between an ordeal and a good sail is attitude."

I recall working with a middle-aged man who suffered from debilitating tinnitus. In his own words, it sounded like "A ton of bricks falling on a pile of church bells... the shock waves blast against my skull...it feels like my brain is gurgling." (Harvey, 1999). He was clearly in a lot of pain; and I was drowning in my empathic pain. Worse yet, his colleagues at work ridiculed him and accused him of malingering. Both he *and I* had recurring fantasies of burning the whole place down with every damn evil person in it: a modern incantation of Sodom and Gomorra. It was only when some colleagues and my therapist helped me to articulate my rage, to discover how it tapped into my issues, and to become more curious about how and why humans can act so evilly toward one another, that I could help him 1) cope with his tinnitus and 2) cope with insensitivity.

Our empathic pain need not be debilitating, "intensified by the imagination and prolonged by a hundred echoes." It need not turn us to stone. By nurturing and giving voice to our curiosity, we can harness some of the wisdom that can be gained from bearing witness to oppression. Our publicly voiced curiosity, even outrage, is not necessarily to change others – although we try – but is for ourselves; it is in the service of our quest for truth; it helps us stay balanced. In the words of Elie Wiesel, "In the beginning, I thought I could change man. Today I know I cannot. If I still shout today, if I still scream, it is to prevent man from ultimately changing me." (Quoted in Brown, 1993).

Admittedly oversimplified, there are three possible consequences of empathy, depending on how one balances the empathic components of cognition and emotion:

1) an imbalance with too much emotion, leading to a loss of boundaries.

2) an imbalance with too much cognition, leading to affective constriction (numbing out).

3) a healthy balance, leading to psychological integration and better interpreting.

References

Brener, A., Riemer, J., & Cutter, W. (1993). *Mourning and Mitzvah: A guided journal for walking the mourner's path through grief and healing.* Vermont: Jewish Lights Pub.

Brown, R.M. (1983). *Elie Wiesel: Messenger to all humanity,* Notre Dame, IN: University of Notre Dame Press, p. 42.

Ciaramicoli, A. P., & Ketcham, K. (2000). *The power of empathy: a practical guide to creating intimacy, self-understanding and love.* New York: Dutton.

Figley, C.R. (1995). *Compassion fatigue: Coping with secondary traumatic stress disorder.* New York: Brunner/Mazel.

Glickman, N.S., & Gulati, S. (2003). *Mental health care of deaf people: A culturally affirmative approach.* Mahwah, NJ: Lawrence Erlbaum Assoc, Pub.

Groopman, J. (1997). *The measure of our days: A spiritual exploration of illness.* New York: Penguin Books.

Harvey, M.A. (1999). *Odyssey of hearing loss: Tales of triumph.* San Diego, CA: Dawn Sign Press.

Harvey, M.A. (2001). *Listen with the heart: Relationships and hearing loss.* San Diego, CA: Dawn Sign Press.

Harvey, M.A. (2003). *Psychotherapy with deaf and hard-of-hearing persons: A systemic model* (second edition). Mahwah, NJ: Lawrence Erlbaum Assoc., Pub.

Lane, H. (1984). *When the mind hears: A history of the deaf.* New York: Random House.

Lane, H., Hoffmeister, R. & Bahan, B. (1996). *A journey into the Deaf world.* San Diego, CA: Dawnsign Press.

Pearlman, L. A., & Saakvitne (1995). *Trauma and the therapist.* New York: W. W. Norton.

Pollard, R. Q. (1998). Personal communication.

Sample Forms Appendix

- Sample Interpreting Resume

- Sample Management Resume

- Team Interpreting Sample Form

- TOSA Template

- Interpreter Request Form

Tammera J. Richards, CI & CT; SC:L; NAD IV

Address Here
(503) Phone Here (V) Business
tjrichards1@msn.com (home e-mail)

tjrichards@tmo.blackberry.net (pager/e-mail)

CERTIFIED SIGN LANGUAGE INTERPRETER

Dually, nationally certified American Sign Language/English interpreter/transliterator specializing in sign-to-voice, mental health, legal, and theatrical/platform settings.

KEY SKILLS AND AREAS OF EXPERIENCE:

- Sign-to-voice interpretation
- Medical interpretation
- Theatrical/platform interpretation

- Conference interpreting

- Mental health/treatment settings
- Legal interpretation
- Interpreter coordination/ business development

- High Tech & IT Interpretation

Education/Certification

National Registry of Interpreters for the Deaf: Specialist Certificate: Legal (SC:L)	January 2004
National Registry of Interpreters for the Deaf Certificate of Transliteration (CT)	June 1995
National Registry of Interpreters for the Deaf Certificate of Interpretation (CI)	August 1994
National Association of the Deaf Level IV: Advanced	October 1993

City University, Bellevue, Washington
   Bachelor of Science: Business Administration, General Administration   March 12, 2005
The Juilliard School, New York, New York
   Theatre Access Project: Interpreting for the Theatre Program   June 1999
Portland Community College, Portland, Oregon
   Sign Language Interpretation Program - September, 1990 - June, 1992
   Internship –Close-up Foundation, SLA, Inc., Washington, D.C., April 1992
   Associate of Applied Sciences Degree – Sign Language Interpretation   June 1992

Work Experience

Video Relay Interpreter   February, 2006-Present
Sorenson Communications

Provide Sign-to-Voice and Voice-to-Sign interpreting/transliterating services via Videophone (VP) technology; involved in mentoring and training newly recruited video interpreters; responsible for evaluating potential Video Interpreter-Provisional (VI-P) candidates; provide technical interpreting services at Salt Lake City headquarters; serve as Point-of-contact (POC) when requested; provide recruiting feedback and support to current manager; promote the overall success of the Portland, Oregon VRS center. Recognized as the go-to person for technical issues and interpreting expertise in the Portland center.

VRI Program Developer/Video Interpreter/Float (Floor Supervisor)   2004-2006
SignOn! (Oregon and Seattle) Video Relay Service (Sprint/CSD)

Provide Sign-to-Voice and Voice-to-Sign interpreting/transliterating services via Video Conferencing technology; Maintain strict consumer confidentiality; Participate in opportunities to upgrade performance; Comply with policies and procedures as outlined by CSD/SignOn Contract; Promote the overall success of the VRS Center. Supervise video interpreters and monitor call center floor dynamics. Communicate with other VRS centers, manage VI breaks, lunches, and handle requisite paperwork, documentation and call issues that may arise. Develop VRI program from the ground up including customer development, technical development and hiring.

Freelance Sign Language Interpreter   1990-Present
NorthWest American Sign Language Associates, Inc.
Provide freelance interpretation services in a variety of settings such as: mental health, medical, legal, professional business, high-tech, social service, post secondary educational, performing arts, political, etc.

Owner/Interpreter Coordinator   1994-1999
NorthWest American Sign Language Associates, Inc.
Owned and managed a sign language interpreter referral service that provided sign language, oral, deaf-blind (tactile) interpreting services to Deaf and hard-of-hearing consumers. Services included daily interpreter referral, emergency on-call services, and ADA consultation.

Staff/Contract Interpreter and Program Assistant   1993-2003
Columbia River Mental Health Services
Provided interpreting services and coordinated interpreting services for a variety of mental health clients with diverse diagnoses, as well as working with Deaf and hearing professional therapists, psychiatrists, nurse practitioners and prescribers. Services provided to a wide range of clients from young children to older adults.

Theatrical Interpreter   1993-Present
Provided translation and interpretation for over 50 productions at the following theatres: Portland Center Stage, Portland, Oregon (10 seasons), Oregon Shakespeare Festival, Ashland, Oregon, Tygres Heart Shakespeare Company, Oregon Children's Theatre, Portland, Oregon, Tulane Summer Shakespeare Festival, New Orleans, Louisiana, Theatre Access Project: Broadway, New York, New York.

Interpreter II   1989-1994
Portland Community College
Provided interpreting services at the college level when needed at varieties of levels and subject matter.

Conferences
Conference Interpreter
Full-time Conference Interpreter, National Registry of Interpreters for the Deaf
Conference 2007
San Francisco, California August, 2007

Conference Interpreter
Full-time Conference Interpreter, National Registry of Interpreters for the Deaf
Conference 2005
San Antonio, Texas July, 2005

Conference Interpreter
Full-time Conference Interpreter, Washington State Registry of Interpreters for the Deaf Conference 2004
Spokane, Washington October, 2004

Conference Interpreter
Full-time Conference Interpreter, Region III Conference 2004
Indianapolis, Indiana July, 2004

Conference Interpreter
Full-time Conference Interpreter, Region V Conference 2004
Portland, Oregon, April, 2004

Conference Interpreter
Full-time Conference Interpreter, Texas Society of Interpreters for the Deaf Conference 2004, San Antonio, Texas, March, 2004

Interpreter Coordinator, NorthWest American Sign Language Associates, Inc. for the President's Committee on Employment of People with Disabilities Conference Portland, Oregon, May, 1995 – provided coordination of interpreting services to over 200 Deaf attendees for this conference.

Publications

♦ "*Establishing A Freelance Interpretation Business: Professional Guidance for Sign Language Interpreters.*" First Edition published May, 1995. Second Edition, 1998. Third Edition due out early 2008.
♦ Team Interpreting: The Team Approach. *Journal of Interpretation*. August, 1993.
♦ Team Interpreting: The Team Approach. *RID Views*. April, 1994.

Professional Memberships

♦ National Registry of Interpreters for the Deaf
♦ National Association of the Deaf
♦ Washington State Registry of Interpreters for the Deaf
♦ Washington State Association of the Deaf

SPECIAL PROJECTS

♦ MSL: Microsoft Sign Language: Participated with a colleague and several Deaf employees in the development and creation of a DVD dictionary and definitions listing of terminology specific to Microsoft Corporation through Microsoft Corporate Diversity.

Presentations/Workshops

♦ Business Practices for Sign Language Interpreters Billing, Collections and Marketing – Oh My! This course focuses on elements of professional business practices in a service industry. While interpreters commonly provide freelance interpretation services, interpreter training programs are woefully lacking in providing foundations in business to allow interpreters to manage their careers professionally and effectively.

Tammera J. Richards, CI & CT; SC:L; NAD IV

Address Here
(503) Phone Here (V) Business
tjrichards1@msn.com (home e-mail)
tjrichards@tmo.blackberry.net (pager/e-mail)

CERTIFIED SIGN LANGUAGE INTERPRETER

Professional sign language interpreter with over 18 years experience in the interpreting field, including over three years experience in VRS settings; Built from the ground up, owned, and operated a successful community interpreter referral service, as well as created and managed a nationwide video remote interpreting system from concept to implementation.

KEY SKILLS AND AREAS OF EXPERIENCE:

- Exceptional technical expertise
- One of only five SC:L holders in Oregon
- Business Development
- Recruiting and training
- Published Author
- Project Management and Implementation
- Mentorship and Evaluation
- People Management

Work Experience

Video Relay Interpreter   **February, 2006-Present**
Sorenson Communications
Provide Sign-to-Voice and Voice-to-Sign interpreting/transliterating services via VP technology; involved in mentoring and training newly recruited video interpreters; responsible for evaluating potential VI-P candidates; provide technical interpreting services at Salt Lake City headquarters; serve as Point-of-contact (POC) when requested; provide recruiting feedback and support to current manager; promote the overall success of the Portland, Oregon VRS center. Recognized as the go-to person for technical issues and interpreting expertise in the Portland center.

Video Remote Interpreting (VRI) Program Specialist   **2005-2006**
SignOn-Oregon, LLC
Responsible for VRI program development, implementation, strategic planning, and customer generation. Built existing program from the ground up including managing and hiring technical staff, testing, and evaluating equipment. Current program is still operating in Seattle, Washington.

Video Interpreter/Floor Supervisor   **2004-2006**
SignOn! Video Relay Service (Sprint/CSD)
Provided Sign-to-Voice and Voice-to-Sign interpreting/transliterating services via video conferencing technology; monitored video interpreters, handled customer service complaints and commendations, troubleshot technical problems, provided administrative assistance to the video interpreter manager, filled out applicable paperwork and maintained call center operations. Reviewed, selected, and trained employees on web-based scheduling system used for video relay center scheduling.

Freelance Sign Language Interpreter   **1989-Present**
NorthWest American Sign Language Associates, Inc.
Provide freelance interpretation services in a variety of settings such as: mental health, medical, legal, professional business, social service, post secondary educational, performing arts (over 50 performances), local, national and regional conferences (including RID 2005 and 2007), and high-tech. Worked for three years as a preferred contract interpreter at Microsoft Corporation in Redmond, WA where I participated with Microsoft Corporate Diversity and Deaf employees in the development and creation of a DVD sign language dictionary (called MSL: Microsoft Sign Language) and terminology listing specific to Microsoft.

Owner/Interpreter Coordinator 1994-1999
NorthWest American Sign Language Associates, Inc.
Built from the ground up, a sign language interpreter referral service that provided sign language, oral and deaf-blind (tactile) interpreting services to Deaf and hard-of-hearing consumers. Services included daily interpreter referral, emergency on-call services, and ADA consultation. Responsible for all aspects of business management including: recruitment, management, mentoring and evaluation of over 50 contractors; acquisition of new business, managing over 500 hours of interpreting services per month including scheduling, billing, accounting and collections. NW ASL was proud to have won the bid to provide sign language interpreting services for over 200 Deaf attendees at the 1995 President's Committee on Employment of People with Disabilities Conference. Sold this successful business in 1999 and it is still a booming business today. Provide expert consultation and evaluation of new interpreters as needed to current owner.

Staff/Contract Interpreter and Program Assistant 1993-2003
Columbia River Mental Health Services
Provided interpreting services and coordinated interpreting services for a variety of mental health clients with diverse diagnoses, as well as working with Deaf and hearing professional therapists, psychiatrists, and nurse practitioners.

TRS Relay Operator 1990-1992
Oregon Relay Service, Portland, Oregon
Provided traditional text-based TTY relay call services to hearing, hard-of-hearing, speech-impaired, and all other users of the Oregon Relay Service while it was based in Portland, OR.

Education/Certification
National Registry of Interpreters for the Deaf: Specialist Certificate: Legal (SC:L)   **January 2004**
National Registry of Interpreters for the Deaf Certificate of Transliteration (CT)   **June 1995**
National Registry of Interpreters for the Deaf Certificate of Interpretation (CI)   **August 1994**
National Association of the Deaf Level IV: Advanced   **October 1993**

City University of Seattle, Bellevue, Washington
   Bachelor of Science: Business Administration, General Administration   **March 2005**
The Juilliard School, New York, New York
   Theatre Access Project: Interpreting for the Theatre Program   **June 1999**
Portland Community College, Portland, Oregon
   Sign Language Interpretation Program - September, 1990 - June, 1992
   Associate of Applied Sciences Degree – Sign Language Interpretation   **June 1992**

Publications

♦ *"Establishing A Freelance Interpretation Business: Professional Guidance for Sign Language Interpreters."* First Edition published May, 1995. Second Edition, 1998. Third Edition due out early 2008.
♦ Team Interpreting: The Team Approach. *Journal of Interpretation.* August, 1993.
♦ Team Interpreting: The Team Approach. *RID Views.* April, 1994.

Presentations/Workshops

♦ Business Practices for Sign Language Interpreters Billing, Collections and Marketing – Oh My! This course focuses on elements of professional business practices in the field of sign language interpretation. The focus of this course is foundations of business, which allows interpreters to manage their careers professionally and effectively.

♦ Legal Terminology for the VRS Interpreter This course focuses on specific legal terminology that may arise during VRS calls. Context and meaning is discussed as well as potential options for interpretation.

References and Protfolio Available Upon Request

TEAM INTERPRETING SAMPLE FORM

1. How long is the total interpreting assignment, from start to finish?

2. What kind of interpretation is required (i.e. ASL, Oral, PSE, SEE, Tactile)?

3. Does the content of the assignment contain a great deal of technical vocabulary, acronyms, and/or specific field-related references?

4. Will technical information, outlines, curriculum, presentations be available for review prior to the interpreting assignment? (Preparation is billed at ____ the interpreter's hourly rate, per hour).

5. Will there be any reading from text during the assignment?

6. Are any breaks scheduled during the course of the assignment, or is the assignment constant/non-stop? Define the amount of break time the interpreter requires.

7. Will there be any media presentations during the assignment (i.e., slides, videotapes that are not captioned, films, or audio media)?

8. Is a deaf individual or individuals presenting during the assignment?

9. Will the assignment be videotaped?

10. Does/do the client(s) have any special needs or requirements (i.e., color of clothing, male/female interpreter preference, tunnel vision, etc.)?

TERMS OF SERVICES AGREEMENT

SCOPE OF WORK: This document constitutes the terms of services agreement for provision of sign language interpreting services by _____ ____ sign language interpreter.

RATES OF PAY: Unless otherwise negotiated in advance, the regular daily rate of payment from 8 AM-5 PM M-F will consist of a $_____ initial fee and then $_____per hour billable in _____ hour increments thereafter.

Unless otherwise negotiated in advance, the after hours' 5 PM-8 AM M-F and 24 hours' rate Saturday and Sunday will consist of a $_____ initial fee and then $_____ per hour billable in ____ hour increments thereafter.

Unless otherwise negotiated in advance, legal interpreting assignments will consist of a $_ _____ initial fee and then $_____ per hour billable in _____ hour increments thereafter. ANY legal assignments, regardless of length, that will include deaf witness testimony will require a team interpreter to ensure accuracy of the record.

TEAM INTERPRETNG POLICY: A team interpreter will be provided for any job assignment that is 1.5 hours or more in length unless otherwise negotiated in advance. The interpreter reserves the right to negotiate a team interpreter for assignments less than 1.5 hours in length should an individual job warrant a team. Should a team of two interpreters have been expected and/or warranted and is not provided, contractor reserves the right to either charge double for work performed or work half the scheduled time without the requisite team in order to prevent injury from occurring, whichever works best to the benefit of both contracting parties.

TRAVEL TIME: Travel that is more than ____ hour in length round-trip, will be billed at _____ the interpreter's hourly rate per hour of travel unless otherwise negotiated.
CANCELLATION POLICY: Unless otherwise negotiated in advance, required notice for cancellation of interpretation/transcription services are as follows:

ASSIGNMENT LENGTH:
1-2 hours   48 weekday hours' notice.
3-5 hours   72 weekday hours' notice.
6-8 hours   96 weekday hours' notice.

Cancellation policy for multiple day assignments will be negotiated on a per assignment basis. Weekday hours are defined as 24 hours Monday through Friday. Should cancellation of assignment not fall within these deadlines, the time booked will be billed for in full.

LATE FEES/PENALTIES:
All invoices are due no later than _____ days from the date of invoice. If an invoice remains outstanding more than _____ days past the date of the invoice then an additional invoice will be submitted with a $_____ late fee; for each additional _____ days the invoice remains outstanding, an additional $_____ late fee will be incurred.

INDEPENDENT CONTRACTOR CERTIFICATION:

_____

is an independent contractor and meets the following criteria for independent contractor status as defined by the IRS:

- ☑ ONLY works pursuant to written contracts.
- ☑ Works in more than three locations in a calendar year.
- ☑ Has a telephone and/or office listing that is separate from one's residence.
- ☑ Purchases advertising or business cards promoting one's business.

PAYMENT SCHEDULE:
All payments will be made payable to: _____EIN/SSN: _____

_____   _____
Your Name Here   Contracting Entity

AGREEMENT TO CONTRACT FOR SERVICES:

I agree to contract for sign language interpretation services with _____
_____ under the outlined terms of service. I understand that this agreement constitutes the full agreement under which both the service provider and requester are bound. This agreement may be terminated by either party with written thirty (30) day notice to the other party informing the other of intent to sever the contract.

_____   Date_____
Your Name Here

_____   Date_____
Service Requester

Business Name/Contractor Name
Street Address
City, State, Zip
Phone Number
E-mail Address

INTERPRETER REQUEST FORM

Form Filled Out By:_____

Date:_____ Time:_____

Requester Name:_____ Phone Number:_____ ☎ 📞

Company Name:_____ FAX Number:_____ ☎ 📞

Contact Person:_____ Phone Number:_____

Billing Address:_____

_____

Deaf Consumer(s):_____

_____

Date(s) of Appointment(s):_____

_____

Time(s) of Appointment(s): From:_____ To:_____

_____

Location of Assignment:_____

_____

Purchase Order Number:_____

Assignment Type:_____

Type of Interpreting Requested: ASL ❑   Transliteration ❑   MLS ❑   Oral ❑   Deaf Blind ❑

Special Requests:_____

_____

Fee:_____

_____

Cancellation Policy Sent/Faxed ❑ Date:_____ Time:_____

Confirmations Sent   ❑ Date:_____ Time:_____

The author would like to thank the following individuals for their contributions, support, expertise, and training, without which this book would not have been possible.

Special Thanks to the Following Individuals/Entities for their Contributions:

W. Edward Ingham, Ph.D.
Cleo Arne, CSC
Ms. Judi Webb, CI & CT; IC/TC
Ms. Liska Jewell, CI & CT; IC/TC; OIC:C
Mr. Stefan N. Richards, MBA
Mr. Patrick Q. Fischer
Mr. James C. McKnight, Jr., CSC
Ms. Sandra L. McKnight, CSC
Ms. Darcie LeMieux
Ms. Debiah McKnight, CSC
Ms. Rebecca Robinson, CSC
Mr. Keith W. Schiewe
Mr. and Mrs. Owen and Leola Goans
Ms. Stephanie Greene, CI & CT; NAD Level III
Mr. and Mrs. David & Judy Parmley
Ms. Julie Gebron, CI & CT; NAD Level IV
Ms. Laurie Meyer, MA, CSC, CI & CT
Mr. Ed Alletto, CSC, CI & CT; SC:L; OIC: S/V, V/S
Ms. Elizabeth Shuey-Morgan, MA, CI & CT; SC:L; NAD V, NIC Advanced
Ms. Keri Brewer, CI & CT; SC:L; NAD V

Text References

Frishberg, N. (1990). *Interpreting: An introduction* (Revised edition). Silver Spring, MD: RID Press.

Gebron, J. (2000). *Sign the speech: An introduction to theatrical interpreting.* Hillsboro, OR: Butte Publications.

McCann, I.L., & Pearlman, L.A. (1990). Vicarious traumatization: A framework for understanding the psychological effects of working with victims. *Journal of Traumatic Stress,* 3, 131-149.

Mindess, A., et al. (1999). *Reading between the signs: Intercultural communication for sign language interpreters.* Boston: Intercultural Press.

Tannen, D. (1995). *Talking from 9-5: Men and women at work.* New York: Harper.

Organizations for the Deaf and Hard of Hearing

The National Association of the Deaf (NAD)
http://www.nad.org/site/pp.asp?c=foINKQMBF&b=91587

World Federation of the Deaf (WFD)
http://www.wfdeaf.org/

American Sign Language Teachers' Association (ASLTA)
http://www.aslta.org/

Post-Secondary Educational Institutions for the Deaf and Hard of Hearing

Gallaudet University
http://www.gallaudet.edu/

National Technical Institute for the Deaf (NTID)
http://www.ntid.rit.edu/

California State University at Northridge
http://www.csun.edu/

Legal Resources for the Deaf and Hard of Hearing

The Deaf Counseling, Advocacy and Referral Agency (DCARA)
http://www.dcara.org/

Greater Los Angeles Agency on Deafness (GLAD)
http://www.gladinc.org/

California Center for Law and the Deaf (CCLD)
http://www.deaflaw.org/

Other Deaf-Oriented Websites of Interest

U.S. Deaf Ski and Snowboarders Association
http://www.usdssa.org/

Deaf Zone – A collection of on-line resources
http://www.deafzone.com/welcome/

Deaf.com
http://www.deaf.com/

Deaf Connect – worldwide Deaf directory
http://www.deafconnect.com/

Deaf Theatre, Interpreted Theatre and Performance Websites

National Theatre of the Deaf (NTD)
http://www.ntd.org/

Deaf West Theatre
http://www.deafwest.org/

Cleveland Signstage Theatre
http://www.signstage.org/

The Deaf Performance Artist Network (D-PAN)
http://www.d-pan.com/index.html

The Theatre Access Project (New York City)
Juilliard Interpreting for the Theatre Program
http://www.tdf.org/
http://www.tdf.org/TDF_ServicePage.aspx?id=70&%20do=v

HandsOn – Theatre Access in New York City
http://handson.org/frames_index.html

Legal Interpreting Resources

The Professional Court Interpreters of San Diego
Hosted by Pasch McCombs, CI & CT; SC:L; NAD V; NIC: Master
http://www.geocities.com/paschmcc/PCISD.html

Court Interpreter Training Resources
Hosted by Carla Mathers, Esq., CSC, SC:L
http://www.carlamathers.net/page1.php
- Sign Language Interpreters in Court: Understanding Best Practices
By Carla Mathers, Esq. CSC, SC:L, ISBN #: 1-4259-2341-0

Conference of Legal Sign Language Interpreters (CLSLI)
http://www.clsli.org/

The Bilingual Courtroom: Court Interpreters in the Judicial Process
By Susan Berk-Seligson ISBN: 978-0-226-04378-4

General Interpreting Resources

The Interpreter's Friend
Hosted by David Bar-Tzur, MS, CI & CT
http://www.theinterpretersfriend.com/

Clearview Innovations
Hosted by Stephen Frank, CI & CT
http://www.clearviewinnovations.com/

The Professional Sign Language Interpreter's Handbook
By Linda Humphries, MA, CSC, CI & CT; SC:L; OTC
http://www.interpretinginfo.com/homepg.html

Decisions! Decisions! A Practical Guide for Sign Language Professionals
By Jan Humphrey, CSC, SC:L; NIC: Advanced
http://www.harriscomm.com/catalog/product_info.php?cPath=35_112&
products_id=1394

So You Want to Be an Interpreter 4th Edition
By Jan Humphrey, CSC, SC:L; NIC: Advanced and Bob Alcorn
http://www.harriscomm.com/catalog/product_info.php?cPath=35_112&
products_id=19146

Continuing Education for Interpreters

Signs of Development
Hosted by Lynne Wiesman, MBA, CI & CT; SC:L
http://www.signs-of-development.org/

Bridge Communications
Hosted by David Evans, CI & CT; NIC: Master
http://www.cofda.com/

Sign Language Associates
Professional Development Opportunities
http://www.signlanguage.com/interpreters/profdev.php

The Distance Opportunities for Interpreter Training Center (DO-IT)
http://www.unco.edu/doit/

Project TIEM On-Line
http://www.asl.neu.edu/TIEM.online/

The Language Door
http://www.thelanguagedoor.com/

NOTES

NOTES